LIGHTHOUSE FOR THE DROWNING

ثلاثة أشكال للموت

شكل أول

أنا الذي غرستُها
قبل ثلاث سنوات
شجرة الكينا التي استطال فرعُها
وباتت ظلَّها يُشبِهُني
وترتمي مني داخلي
مضطرباً مرتبكاً مثلي
أنا غرستُها
شجرة الكينا بفرعها الطويل
بفرعها الذي استطالَ،
إنها الحياةْ
وليس لي أنا
سوى عناق ظلِّها الذي يُشبِهُني

LIGHTHOUSE FOR THE DROWNING

Poems by

Jawdat Fakhreddine

Translated from the Arabic by
Huda Fakhreddine and Jayson Iwen

BOA Editions, Ltd. ▧ Rochester, NY ▧ 2017

First Edition
17 18 19 20 7 6 5 4 3 2 1

For information about permission to reuse any material from this book, please contact The
Permissions Company at www.permissionscompany.com or e-mail permdude@gmail.com.

Publications by BOA Editions, Ltd.—a not-for-profit corporation under section 501 (c) (3)
of the United States Internal Revenue Code—are made possible with funds from a variety of
sources, including public funds from the Literature Program of the National Endowment for
the Arts; the New York State Council on the Arts, a state agency; and the County of Mon-
roe, NY. Private funding sources include the Lannan Foundation for support of the Lannan
Translations Selection Series; the Max and Marian Farash Charitable Foundation; the Mary
S. Mulligan Charitable Trust; the Rochester Area Community Foundation; the Steeple-Jack
Fund; the Ames-Amzalak Memorial Trust in memory of Henry Ames, Semon Amzalak, and
Dan Amzalak; and contributions from many individuals nationwide.

Cover Design: Daphne Morrissey
Cover Art: *Sunset Over Beirut* by Ali Fakhreddine
Interior Design and Composition: Richard Foerster
Manufacturing: McNaughton & Gunn
BOA Logo: Mirko

Library of Congress Cataloging-in-Publication Data

Names: Fakhr al-Dein, Jawdat author. | Fakhreddine, Huda J. translator. |
  Iwen, Jayson, 1974– translator. | Fakhreddine, Jawdat. Poems. Selections.
  English. | Fakhreddine, Jawdat. Poems. Selections.
Title: Lighthouse for the drowning : poems / by Jawdat Fakhreddine ;
  translated from the Arabic by Huda Fakhreddine and Jayson Iwen.
Description: First edition. | Rochester, NY : BOA Editions, Ltd., 2017. | In English and
  Arabic. | Originally published in 1996 under the title: Manearah lil-ghareiq.
Identifiers: LCCN 2016049058 | ISBN 9781942683391 (pbk. : alk. paper)
Classification: LCC PJ7824.A363 A2 2017 | DDC 892.7/16—dc23 LC record
available at https://lccn.loc.gov/2016049058

Lannan

BOA Editions, Ltd.
250 North Goodman Street, Suite 306
Rochester, NY 14607
www.boaeditions.org
A. Poulin, Jr., Founder (1938–1996)

Contents

Introduction

When *Manaraton lil ghariq* (*A Lighthouse for the Drowning*) was pub-lished in 1996, its critical reception established Jawdat Fakhreddine as one of the most consequential of the second generation Arab Mod-ernist poets. Though Fakhreddine had published five well-regarded collections of poetry prior to *Lighthouse*, the general consensus was that with *Lighthouse* he had achieved a breakthrough not only in his personal style but for the poetic language of his generation. By the middle of the twentieth century, Arabic poets were generally aligning themselves with one of two camps; they either modeled their work after the Classical Arabic tradition or rebelled against that tradition in a manner consistent with the values of the international Modernist movement. In response to this situation, Fakhreddine and his con-temporaries began searching for ways to balance foreign imperatives with those of the Classical Arabic tradition, and the appearance of *Lighthouse* introduced a new way to do so.

To help readers unfamiliar with the Arabic poetic tradition gain a better understanding of Fakhreddine's accomplishment, we will highlight several characteristics of *Lighthouse* that would not likely be noticeable otherwise. The first is that nearly every poem in the book begins with an allusion to a Classical Arabic poem, some-times a poem that has become almost commonplace in daily Arabic parlance. Fakhreddine then personalizes and adapts the spirit of that poem to the conditions of his own life. One could say, in a sense, that he translates the formal, Classical poem into an informal, private confession, in language that eschews affectation and pretense. The result is something like an anthology of intimately innovative cover songs that have all been performed by Fakhreddine, in his own living space, for the ostensible audience of himself.

The simplicity and intimacy of the verse in *Lighthouse* distinguishes it from contemporary Arabic verse that relies on intentional devices, such as extra-ordinary imagery, rhyme, meter, or typography, to identify itself as poetry. Though the poems in *Lighthouse* do, in fact, employ meter (often the meter of the Classical poems to which they allude), they do so in such a subtle fashion that it wouldn't be readily discernible to casual Arabic readers. Fakhreddine's stated intent with *Lighthouse*, as with his subsequent works, has been to elide form and content, to present poetry as a way of thinking or being, rather than as an object assembled from elements predetermined to be poetic, as is the practice of many poets, Arab and otherwise. *Lighthouse* is essentially an extended meditation on the nature of poetry and its relation to one's experience of time and the material world.

Fakhreddine wrote *Lighthouse* during a period of time that he considered to be the likely center of his lifespan, as implied in the poem "Forty." The book represents a reappraisal of his life and calling, both of which had been significantly altered by then. Fakhreddine had experienced at least three major readjustments in his life prior to the composition of *Lighthouse.* The first occurred in his youth, when his homeland of Southern Lebanon became a theater of war with Israel, causing him to relocate to Beirut, where he began his postsecondary education in the sciences, eventually earning a master's degree in Physics, which he then taught at the high school level for over ten years. During this time, he continued to write and publish poetry, and was encouraged by the poet Adonis to pursue postgraduate work in literature. Adonis's encouragement eventually led to another significant readjustment in his life, from a career in the sciences to one in the arts, ultimately resulting in his attainment of a PhD in Arabic Literature and a professorship at The Lebanese University. His third readjustment occurred during the Lebanese Civil War, when he temporarily emigrated to The United States. It was during this exile in America that Fakhreddine began work on what would eventually become *Lighthouse for the Drowning*, completed five years after his return to Lebanon.

We had initially considered translating a representative selection of Fakhreddine's poetry from across his career, but instead decided to translate the single text of *Lighthouse* in its entirety, first, to pay homage to the significance of the book, and, second, to provide readers a sense of the tone and development of the poems in relation to each other as they accumulated chronologically over this pivotal period in Fakhreddine's life. An unanticipated side effect of our decision to work on poems that had been composed in overlapping psychological states, due to their proximity in time, was that it greatly aided us in our translation, as we will later elaborate.

We encountered all the challenges endemic to translation, foremost among them the inconvenient fact that there is no direct correspondence in meaning between any two words of any two languages, so one will often encounter situations such as we did in the poem "Seas," where the Arabic word "bahr" has a primary meaning of "sea" and a secondary meaning of "meter," making a literal translation not only undesirable but impossible. As daunting as such an obstacle might seem, any resourceful translator can negotiate it with at least tolerable success (in the case of "Seas," we periodically translated "bahr" as "wave(s)," to suggest both rhythm and bodies of water). There is likewise the common challenge of managing language that alludes to cultural information not contained within the work being translated. Given the highly allusive nature of *Lighthouse*, we frequently encountered such language and dealt with it on a case-by-case basis. Sometimes we did so with editorial notes and other times by eliciting cultural cognates to which the English could allude, as we did with the poem "Heavy Essence," which would more literally be translated as something like "Strong Scent," if the title weren't invoking a metaphor from a Classical Arabic poem about the spirit of confidence and pride that can be physically detected in the presence of certain people. And so goes the litany of spells under which all translators labor, in varying degrees of enchantment and torment.

There are, however, challenges unique to the translation of any given pair of languages. When it comes to Arabic and English literature, the translator must also negotiate two distinct sets of aesthetic values that are often mutually incompatible. For the sake of brevity, we will mention only the two we found ourselves negotiating most often: abstraction and repetition. In short, abstraction and repetition, handled artfully, are highly regarded by Arabic audiences, while contemporary English audiences generally seem to find abstraction and repetition annoying, however handled. This occasionally leads to the conundrum of trying to figure out how to do justice to a poem that is savored by Arabic critics for the very reasons it would be unpalatable to English critics. We encountered moments like this in *Lighthouse*, and, though we don't claim to have discovered a magic formula for aligning cultural values, we do feel that we did justice to the work in both languages. How we did so, once again, was through the application of techniques that would undoubtedly sound familiar to many translators. To address what may have been considered abundant abstraction, we were strategic in our synonym selection process, raising figurative motifs, which lay deep beneath the surface of the Arabic text, closer to the surface of the English text. We thereby tried to suggest imagery, which also helped replace meaning that was necessarily lost between the languages (such as the aforementioned allusions to Classical texts, or the meter, which we felt was subtle enough in the original to safely abandon for a more indigenous English free verse rhythm, rather than attempting to approximate the original rhythm and most likely ending up with an affected tone). As for repetition, we replaced what English readers would likely consider excessive verbatim repetition with variations on the themes of the original phrasings, often selecting variations that would reinforce other motifs we had decided to highlight.

This wasn't always our approach. In fact, we have translated the entirety of *Lighthouse for the Drowning* twice now, from scratch. The first time was over a decade ago, when we were both still living in Beirut. At that time, neither of us felt confident enough in our abilities as translators and poets to deviate from a fairly conventional, almost literal, treatment of the language. When we decided to revisit the book a couple years ago, we agreed to honor the original and its Arabic audiences by being more mindful of alternative ways to more effectively elicit similar states in English audiences, by allowing ourselves more liberty with the language. We decided to create a version that approximated the casual fluidity of the original, while still suggesting its depth.

The second time around, our collaborative process went something like this: Huda would produce a scholarly, literal translation of a poem, often including supplementary notes on form, idiom, and cultural reference, being as loyal to the primary meaning of the original as possible. Jayson would then study this draft, with two considerations foremost in mind: 1) what he believed Jawdat Fakhreddine was feeling during the composition of the poem, based on the cumulative tone and texture of the entire manuscript as well as the distinct nuances of the poem under consideration, and 2) how he believed English readers would interpret and understand the sum of the poem. His goal was to bring these two projections as close to one another as possible, by whatever means the poem provided. Thus, Jayson would craft a second draft of the new poem, which was then sent back to Huda, whose job, at that point, was to remain faithful to the Arabic and to explain to Jayson anything that he seemed to have misunderstood. Jayson would listen carefully, ask questions, and advocate on behalf of the English version when it still seemed in the best interest of the poem. This negotiation would continue until both collaborators felt they had been as successful as possible in their respectively assigned roles in the process.

Aside from such technical considerations, we would like to conclude with a brief articulation of the philosophy behind our current approach. It is our belief, born of study and practice, that, in their work, literary writers are usually aiming at something beyond words, something they can never entirely capture, and it was toward that ineffable thing, that distant shape we saw wavering on the horizon of each poem, that we likewise aimed with each translation. We took the originals to be scripts in need of performance by an actor, with that performance being the English poem. Each poem could be performed in an endless variety of ways, each inducing in the audience a different effect. And yet an actor must choose. The translator-actor assumes, as best she can, through empathy and understanding, the perceived character of the author (aided, in this particular case, by the psychological continuity of *Lighthouse*). She then feels the lines course through her, and she stands at the lip of the stage, and, with her own tongue, tries to articulate the vision she sees in the air beyond. This, at least, was our aspiration for *Lighthouse for the Drowning*.

Jayson Iwen & Huda Fakhreddine

LIGHTHOUSE FOR THE DROWNING

Three Profiles of Death

1.
I planted it,
three years ago,
the eucalyptus whose branch has grown
to resemble me.
It shivers within me,
confused and pale
as I.
I planted the tree
whose branching is life
and what have I
but the embrace of a shadow that becomes me?
I see us standing in stark exposure.
We exult and we conceal one another.
One is the shade
while together we are the secret
of our embrace.
This tree is life
and the branch I see reaching
takes me,
returns me to the wild.
It is life
and what am I
but the one
who planted it.

ثلاثة أشكال للموت

. ١

أنا الذي غرستُها
قبل ثلاثِ سنواتْ.
شجرة الكينا التي استطال فرْعُها،
وبات ظلُّها يشبهُني،
ويرتمي في داخلي،
مضطرباً وباهتاً مثلي.
أنا غرستُها
شجرة الكينا بفرعِها الطويلْ.
بفرعِها الذي استطالَ،
إنها الحياةُ.
وليس لي أنا
سوى عناق ظلِّها الذي يشبهُني.
أرى إلينا واقفيْن في عرائنا الشديد،
ننتشي ، أو نحتمي ببعضِنا.
واحدُنا ظلٌّ،
ولكنّا معاً سرُّ عناقِنا الظليلْ.
شجرتي ، هي الحياةُ.
وفرْعُها الذي أراه يستطيلُ يستطيلْ
يأخذُني،
يُطلقُ وجهي في الفلاةْ.
هي الحياةُ.
وما أنا؟
لستُ سوى ...
أنا الذي غرستُها ...

2.
To the one I love
I say: our time together ends
in seconds or in years.
It will end.
If only we could go on in this embrace
and never return.
What holds us back from disappearing
into an encounter whose end
approaches even now?

3.
The poem, which I drafted,
I read.
Then I redrafted it
and read
and read it again,
until I released it
unto listeners
at a reading
and then I forgot it.
Now, when I meet it in a book
from time to time,
it beckons to me like a prisoner,
lets out a sigh
and glows.
It wants to know where I've been.
Whenever I face it,
I face a new meaning
for absence.

(May 1990)

. ٢

أقولُ للتي أحبُّها
سينتهي لقاؤنا بعد قليلْ.
بعد ثوانٍ، أو سنينْ.
سينتهي،
فليتنا نذهبُ في لقائنا ولا نعودُ،
ما الذي يجعلنا لا نتلاشى
في لقائنا الذي سينتهي، بعد قليلْ؟!

. ٣

قصيدتي التي سوَّدْتُها،
قرأتُها.
وبعدما بيَّضْتُها،
قرأتُها ثانيةً.
ثم قرأتُها ثلاثاً ... أربعاً ...
ومرةً ألقيتُها،
ألقيتُها في المهرجانْ.
وبعد هذا كلِّه ، نسيتُها.
وصرتُ كلَّما التقيتُها،
حيناً فحيناً في الكتابْ
هفتْ إليَّ كالسجينِ،
أطلقتْ أنفاسَها،
توهَّجتْ،
وساءلتْني عن غيابي.
كلَّما واجهتُها،
واجهتُ معنىً للغيابْ.

(أيار 1990)

Glow
(To Talal and Haytham)

1.

In the nights that wasted us
we only found tomorrow,
a prey
cowering under the cover of night.
We caressed it with words,
and consoled it with sympathetic song.
All we found in the nights that wasted us
and closed upon our whispering
under the canopy of stars
was tomorrow
trembling,
glowing like prey in the forest of death.

2.

We found in politics,
poems and dictionaries
a feeble spark
for our guttering hearts.
We took refuge in the flame,
fearing it may go out
in the wilderness of nights that wasted us.
It must be yesterday, then
our glistening death.
Illusion, our savior!
It is you we choose,
and in your shadow we stay alight.
You are the branch of life,
and the only ember left
of our extinguished hearts.

توهُّج
(إلى طلال وهيثم)

. ١.

لم نجدْ في الليالي التي أتلفتْنا
سوى غَدِنا،
جانحاً تحت جُنْحِ الليالي،
طريداً،
ونحن نلامسُهُ بالكلامِ ،
نخفِّفُ عنه ببعض الأغاني التي وهنَتْ،
أو ببعض القصائدْ.
لم نجدْ في الليالي التي أتلفتْنا،
وضاقتْ ببثٍّ لنا جانحٍ تحت جُنْحِ الليالي،
سوى غَدِنا،
خائفاً،
يتوهَّجُ في غابة الموت مثلَ الطرائدْ.

. ٢.

لم نجدْ في السياسةِ ،
أو في القصائدْ ،
أو في المعاجمِ ،
إلا بريقاً لأرواحنا المطفآتْ.
فلُذْنا جميعاً به،
وحنوْنا عليه مخافةَ أن ينضوي
في حطام الليالي التي أتلفتْنا.
إذنْ ، إنه أمسُنا،
موتُنا المتوهِّجُ،
فانهضْ بنا أيها الوهْمُ،
أنت الذي نصطفيه ، ونسهرُ في ظلِّهِ ،
أنت غصنُ الحياةْ.
والبريقُ الذي يتبقَّى لأرواحنا المطفآتْ.

3.
We found neither
in politics
nor poems nor dictionaries
nor in the nights that wasted us
anything looming
into our sight.
We retired to our illusions
and sat there turning coals
in the ashes of language.

(December 1990)

. ٣ .

لم نجدْ في الليالي التي أتلفثَنا،

ولا في السياسةِ،

أو في القصائدِ،

أو في المعاجمِ،

شيئاً يلوِّحُ كي نبلُغَهْ.

فأوينا إلى بعض أوهامنا،

وجلسْنا نقلِّبُ جمراً لها في رماد اللغَهْ.

(كانون الأول 1990)

September

1.

There the September garden.
Why do I not leap light
to its bright quivering among the branches?
Why do I not perish in its swaying slumber?
This the September garden.
How do I stand still
against its trembling?
What is it
that awakens in us, me and the garden,
something like words?
Would this air speak?
Had we, the garden and I,
not disintegrated so!

2.

September garden is a day
I put together as I please.
I don't assemble
so much as perish in it,
between what fades
and what takes form.
I abandon myself to the garden.
In a place where there is no day
all ceases, and nothing is left behind
but words.
In the garden of September
nothing is, but everything
speaks.

حديقةُ أيلول

. ١ .

قلتُ : هذي حديقةُ أيلولَ،
كيف إذن لا أهبُّ خفيفاً
إلى موجها المتألق بين الغصونِ؟
ولا أتبدَّدُ في نومها المتراقصِ!
هذي حديقةُ أيلولَ،
كيف أداري وقوفي أمام ارتجافتها؟
قلتُ : هل ثَمَّ شيءٌ
يُحرِّكُ فينا (أنا والحديقةِ)
ما يشبهُ الكلماتْ؟
أينطقُ هذا الهواءُ؟
إذا لم ندعْهُ (أنا والحديقةُ)
ينثرُنا كالشتاتْ!

. ٢ .

حديقةُ أيلولَ يومٌ،
أنظِّمُهُ كيفما أشتهي.
لا أنظِّمُهُ،
بل أزولُ بهِ،
بين ما يضمحلُّ وما يتشكَّلُ،
أمضي بهِ،
إلى حيث لايومَ ، لا وقتَ،
بل كلُّ شيءٍ يزولُ.
ويتركُ قولاً لهُ ...
في حديقة أيلولَ ... لا شيءَ،
بل كلُّ شيءٍ يقولُ.

3.

The garden of September comes to me
and dozes on my sight,
trembling with fatigue
in the small sky,
that which rapturously glitters
on the green leaves,
a sky that drags its robe
over the trees.
September comes to me.
I sit up and face it
with dreamful things:
a book, a pack of cigarettes,
a cup of tea, and a bit of evening
scattered,
surprised and bewildered by the cold.
I face it free and transparent.
I rise to it.
The garden of September,
woven of imaginings,
a temptation like all beginnings.

(9/7/1991)

. ٣ .

حديقةُ أيلولَ تأتي إليَّ،
وتغفو على نظْرتي،
وهْي تـهتَزُّ واهنةً في السماء الصغيرةِ،
تلك التي تتلألأ جذْلى بأعلى الشجيْراتِ،
تسحبُ فوق الشجيْرات أذيالها ...
حديقةُ أيلولَ تأتي إليَّ،
فأنهض في جلستي،
أتصدّى لها، بأشيائيَ الساهماتِ:
كتابٍ ، وعلبة تبغٍ،
وفنجان شايٍ،
وبعض مساءٍ تلاشى من السِّحْرِ،
أغْضى ذهولاً،
فغافلهُ البرْدُ،
شيءٌ من البرْدِ، طَلْقٌ، رقيقٌ،
فأنهض في جلستي،
أتصدّى لها،
لحديقة أيلولَ ، تلك التي نسجَتْها الخيالاتْ.
فتنةٌ مثْلَ كلِّ البداياتْ.

(1991 . 9 . 7)

[25]

Preparation

Before long we leave,
and there will remain what
will tell of us.
All that remains
will tell of us,
of our faces
welcoming the dawn
or alert in the night.
All will speak of us as we retire
to our half nights,
the other halves left
out in the garden.
We leave and our features remain,
our words
and the birds that fluttered
in our cups,
our chairs,
and the trees
speaking into baskets.
Before long we leave
and what we didn't say
and what we have always said
will stay.
We prepare for our own absence.
We gather ourselves,
and yet all that is here
speaks of our having been.
Why then?
Is it because we depart and depart
forever leaving behind
a little of ourselves?

(9/14/1991)

تَهيُّؤ

قليلاً، ونمضي.
ويبقى هنا ما يدلُّ علينا.
هنا، كلُّ ما يتبقَّى يدلُّ علينا،
أساريرُنا حين نستقبلُ الفجرَ،
أو حين نسمَرُ،
أو حين نأوي إلى نصف ليلتنا،
ونُخلِّفُ نصفاً لها في الحديقةِ،
نمضي وتبقى أساريرُنا،
وأحاديثُنا،
والطيورُ التي خفقتْ في فناجين قهوتنا،
والكراسيُّ،
والشجراتُ التي نطقتْ في السلالِ،
قليلاً ، ونمضي.
ويبقى الذي لم نقُلْهُ ، وقلناهُ دوْماً،
نُعِدُّ إذن للرحيلِ،
نُهيِّءُ أنفسنا،
غيرَ أنّ هنا كل شيءٍ يدلُّ علينا.
لماذا إذن؟
ألأنّا نغيبُ نغيبُ ...
ويبقى هنا ما يدلُّ علينا؟

(1991 . 9 . 14)

[27]

Foxes

The foxes cry out their sayings.
How I love listening to them!
How they console me at dusk!
Every evening, their howls
become a cloud of childhood whims,
of golden little hopes.
I greet their voices
like a child.
Whenever I come here
the foxes come to me,
these cherished memories
that resurrect me.
Like a child I listen,
and the foxes speak.
More than thirty five years
I still hear them when I'm here.
They still lure me to a summer,
small as the waves of childhood,
tender as the glitter of promise.
Here I am for more than thirty-five years
speaking, yet without words.
How I love listening to my brothers, the foxes, this evening . . .
The foxes speak.

(9/15/1991)

ثعالب

تقولُ الثعالبُ أقوالها ...
كم أحبُّ استماعي إليها،
وتؤنسُني أوّلَ الليلِ،
كلَّ مساءٍ ألاقي بأصواتها عَبَقاً من جموح الطفولةِ،
من ذَهَب الأمنيات الصغيرةِ،
كلَّ مساءٍ أقابلُ أصواتها فرحاً مثلَ طفلٍ.
هنا ، كلّما جئتُ،
تأتي إليَّ الثعالبُ كالذكريات الحبيبةِ،
تبعثُني،
كلّما جئتُ أصغي إليها كطفلٍ.
تقولُ الثعالبُ أقوالها ...
منذ أكثر من خمسة وثلاثينَ عاماً،
وما زلتُ أسمعُها كلّما جئتُ،
تخطفُني نحو صيف صغيرٍ،
صغير كموج الطفولةِ،
غضّ كبارقة الأمنيات الصغيرةِ،
ها إنني منذ أكثر من خمسة وثلاثينَ عاماً
أقولُ ، ولا قولَ لي.
كم أحبُّ استماعي إلى صحْبتي من ثعالب هذا المساء ...
... تقولُ الثعالبُ أقوالها ...

(1991 . 9 . 15)

Seas[1]

(To Talal and Haytham)

1.

Seas . . . distant seas,
my spirit was like them
before the water broke my sight,
before the spreading numbness crept into my stride,
before new murmurs slipped into my solitude.

2.

Seas . . . seas . . .
to poetry are distant seas,
far away yet closer than the shores dare say,
deeper than the skies confess,
a wave for every new thing,
a wave for every old.
Poetry is the deepest sea,
distant yet more urgent than surf breaking on rocks.
A balcony
a book and a table.
We came to them
and the waves of poetry washed over us.[2]
Our papers were carried away by clouds
that rose from the "mothers of poems."[3]

---

[1] The word "sea" is a translation of the Arabic word "bahr," which also means a meter of poetry. "Buhur al-Shi 'r" (the meters of poetry) were discovered, or rather derived, from Arabic poetry, by al-Khalīl b. Aḥmad al-Farāhīdī.

[2] "Waves" here is our rendering of the names of meters in the Arabic original: al-basīt (simple), al-ṭawīl (long), and al-khafīf (light).

[3] "Umahāt al-qaṣā'd" (the mothers of poems) is an Arabic phrase used to refer to the most beautiful of poems. It often refers to poems by major Pre-Islamic and Abbasid poets. Another similar phrase is "'Uyūn al-Shi'r" (the eyes of poetry).

بُحُور
(إلى طلال وهيثم)

. ١ .

بُحورٌ ... بُحورٌ بعيدهْ.
... وكنتُ أرى هِمّتي مثلَها،
قبل أن يكسرَ الماءُ من نظرتي،
قبل أن يسريَ الكَدَرُ المتطاوِلُ في خطوتي،
قبل أن تتسرّبَ في وحشتي همهماتٌ جديدهْ.

. ٢ .

بُحورٌ بُحورْ.
وللشعرِ أبعدُ منها،
وأقربُ مما تقولُ الشواطئُ،
أعمقُ مما تقولُ السماواتُ،
بحرٌ لكلّ جديد
وبحرٌ لكلّ قديمٍ
وللشعرِ أبعدُ من كلّ بحرٍ
وأقربُ من لُجّة تتكسّرُ فوق الصخورْ.
بُحورٌ بُحورْ ...
جعلنا لها شرفةً ، وكتاباً ، وطاولةً،
وجلسنا إليها،
فخفَّ إلينا الطويلُ ، البسيطُ ، الخفيفُ ...
وطارتْ بأوراقنا سُحُبٌ،
طالعتنا بها أمّهاتُ القصائدْ.

[31]

We divided them among us
at a table, for vision not study,
and we said: this is the secret of secrets,
this is our quest.
Let us play this game
at our unsteady table.
Seas, distant seas
and this Khalil[4] who died a thousand years ago
dies and rises,
dies and is buried every day,
but lives again.
Life issues forth
like daily papers.

3.
Seas . . . seas . . .
to poetry is a sea deeper than any other sea,
farther than any other,
yet closer than waves breaking on the rocks.
Seas . . . seas . . .
And on the shores we drown.
This is our age,
a raging ox.

(November 1991)

---

[4] A reference to al-Khalīl b. Aḥmad mentioned above. The word "khalīl" means friend.

نشَرْنا القصائدَ ما بيننا،
فوق طاولة للتصوُّر، لا للبحوث،
وقلْنا : هنا سِرُّ أسرارنا،
وهنا البحثُ،
فلْنلعبِ الآن لعبتَنا،
فوق طاولة للشدائدْ.
بُحورٌ بُحورٌ...
وهذا (الخليل) الذي مات من ألف عام،
يموتُ ويحيا،
يموتُ ويُدفنُ في كلِّ يوم ... ويحيا،
... ،وتجري الحياةُ
فتصدُرُ يوماً فيوماً،
صدورَ الجرائدْ.

. ٣ .

بُحورٌ بُحورْ.
وللشعرِ أعمقُ من كلِّ بحرٍ
وأبعدُ من كلِّ بحرٍ
وأقربُ من لُجّةٍ تتكسّرُ فوق الصخورْ.
بُحورٌ بُحورْ ...
ونحن على الشطِّ غرْقى،
وهذا هو العصْرُ،
ثورٌ يَخورْ.

(تشرين الثاني 1991)

Do I Take Refuge in Myself?

1.

For how long will I take refuge in myself
when all I fend off
hides between my eyes
like the mark of a purebred stallion,
when all I defeat
seems to mock me
or smirk behind my back?
In the past, I imagined
a fortress that would be my sanctuary,
when I rise, when I sleep,
when in the crowds
my shadow roams.
The idea protected me awhile,
and then I lost it.
This is how I have hidden in myself.
I lost my ease a long time ago.
I lost my pace.
Fear is a friend that flatters me.
It alone pities me.
It alone becomes restless in my loneliness.
A brother for the road,
when I walk alone.

هل ألوذُ بنفسي؟

إلامَ ألوذُ بنفسي؟

وكلُّ الذي أتّقيهِ بها

ثابتٌ بين عينيَّ وشْماً أصيلاً،

كوشْم حصانٍ أصيلٍ.

إلامَ ألوذُ بنفسي؟

وكلُّ الذي أتّقيهِ،

يُلوِّحُ لي ساخراً،

أو يُقهْقِهُ في أثَري.

من زمانٍ، هفوتُ إلى فكرةٍ حول حصنٍ،

يكون ملاذي إذا قمْتُ، أو نِمْتُ،

أو هامَ في الناس ظِلّي.

هفوتُ إلى فكرةٍ، حصَّنتْني قليلاً، وضيَّعْتُها ...

هكذا كنتُ دوْماً ألوذُ بنفسي.

فقدْتُ الرِّضى من زمانٍ،

أضعْتُ خُطايَ،

شعرتُ بخوفي خليلاً، يُجاملُني.

وحدَهُ يترفّقُ بي،

وحدَهُ يتململُ في وحدتي،

وحدَهُ، حين أمشي،

يسيرُ أخاً لطريقي.

2.

Until when will I take refuge in myself,
when my time has slipped away,
between avoidance and refrain?
There it is, still sneaking away,
like a prey.
I meet my past days.
I envy their survival,
and I sympathize with the days to come.
I pity them if they stay too long.
Time is holding its breath,
so how much longer can I hide in myself?

(1/20/1992)

. ٢ .

إلامَ ألوذُ بنفسي؟

وقد دَلَفَ العمرُ بين تَحاش هنا، وتَلاف هناكِ،

وها هو ما زال ينسلُّ بين الكُوى،

يتسلَّلُ مثلَ الطريدِ،

أقابلُ أيامِيَ الماضياتِ، فأغبطُها أن نَجَتْ،

ثم أحنو على القادماتِ حُنُوّاً،

وأُشفقُ أن تتطاولَ ...

قد حَبَسَ العمرُ أنفاسَهُ،

فإلامَ ألوذُ بنفسي؟

(1992 . 1 . 20)

For Yemen

1.
As if on the verge of a new beginning,
I walk and the mountains approach,
the cloud mountains rumbling around me.
As if in these virgin fields
I summon from the hidden nectar
a soul for my weary days,
as if I were retrieving waters from lost springs,
flowing outward along forgotten paths.
Clouds rise in the space of my soul,
now awakened.
A luminescence in the earth here releases the clouds, the mountains,
and draws the distant skies near, then tosses them onto the wasteland
that blooms elated in sun and shadow.
Mountains naked as gods,
they are the scattering of the desert,
the fallen robes of the sky.
Mountains like fathers who bow their heads
so their sons may triumph over fear and death
and the paths that end
in the impossible horizon.

قصيدة إلى اليمن

.١.

كأني في مَهَبّ أوّلٍ،
أمشي، فتقتربُ الجبالْ.
تُدمدمُ حوليَ السُحُبُ الجبالْ.
كأني في الفيافي البِكْرِ،
أقبِضُ من رحيق غائرٍ،
روحاً لأيامي التي وهَنَتْ.
كأني أستعيدُ لنفسيَ الماءَ الذي ضاعتْ أوائلُهُ،
وأفلتَ بعد ذلك في مجاريه التي ضيَّعْتُها.
سُحُبٌ تعالتْ في فضاءِ الروحِ،
روحي بعدما انتفضتْ .
هنا للأرض برقٌ يبعثُ السُحُبَ الجبالْ.
ويجتذبُ السماوات البعيدةَ،
ثم يُلْقيها على القفْر الذي يُغْضي
طَروباً للشموس وللظلالْ.
جبالٌ مثلُ آلهة عُراةٍ،
هُمْ نُثارُ القفْرِ،
أثوابُ السماواتِ التي هبطتْ.
جبالٌ مثلُ آباء حذَوْا هاماتِهِمْ
زُلْفى لأبناء لَهُمْ
كي يستقرّوا فوق هاماتِ الردى، والهوْلِ،
والسُبُلِ التي تنْسَدُّ في أُفُقِ المُحالْ.

Unvanquished mountains.
People have set up their houses there
so they may rise into disappearance.
They fade into the looming heights
as if their homes were veils they've drawn across the mountain peaks.
It is as if I were on the verge of emerging myths.
Who roused horror in these craning peaks,
then humbled it
and bestowed upon it this charm?
A bewildering halo quivers over the plateaus.
Fallen stars are the whims of the wild.
They tell of nature's greed, as it rises, of rocks
in the space that defies death on mountain tops.
As if I were on the verge of myths newborn,
walking in footsteps familiar for a thousand years,
following a familiar light for as long,
I seize the retreating spirit
and scatter it.
The mountains embrace it.
The cloud mountains fly heavy with my soul.

جبالٌ لا تُنالْ.

أرسى أُناسٌ فوقها سَكَناً لَهُمْ

حتى يغيبوا في غيابٍ شاهقٍ.

لاحتْ أعاليهمْ وهمْ غابوا،

كأنَّ بيوتَهُمْ حُجُبٌ أقاموها على قِمَمِ الجبالْ.

كأني في مَهَبٍّ للأساطيرِ الوليدةِ،

مَنْ أثار الرُّعْبَ في هذي الوعورِ المُشْرَئِبّةِ؟

ثم ذلَّلَهُ،

وألْقى فوقه سِحْراً،

فماجتْ هالةٌ مذهولةٌ فوق الشِّعابِ،

كأنها شُهبٌ تُحدّثُ عن جموح الوعْرِ،

عن نَهَمِ الطبيعةِ وهْي تصعَدُ،

عن صخورٍ للفضاءِ المُستميتِ على الجبالْ.

كأني في مَهَبٍّ للأساطيرِ الوليدةِ،

أنقُلُ الخطْوَ الذّي يعتادُني من ألفِ عامٍ،

أتبَعُ البرقَ الذي يعتادُني من ألفِ عامٍ،

أقبِضُ الروحَ التي انقبضتْ،

وأذْروها،

فتحضُنُها الجبالْ.

وتطيرُ مُثْقَلَةً بِها السُحُبُ الجبالْ.

2.

Time is one long *maqīl*.[5]
Its plant circulates among us.
It beckons us into its weary shade
and tends to us like a mother.
But the howling,
the howling that arrives from our frail extremes
and throws itself into the plant's branches,
quivers there until the plant bends.
It clouds two or three times
and then rains in the corners of our *maqīl*.
How does the plant cloud or rain?
And why does it tend to us like a mother?
Does it break out of the language of howling?

---

[5] The "maqīl" is an afternoon gathering which goes on until after sunset. It is a part of Yemen's daily routine. People usually gather to chew qāt, which is a plant that has certain alerting effects (like coffee or tea). However, in some cases, the gathering for qāt turns into an intellectual gathering where politics and art are often discussed. Poetry is sometimes read in such gatherings as well.

. ٢.

مَقيلٌ واحدٌ هذا الزمانُ،

تدورُ نبتتُهُ علينا،

تصطفينا تحت أفياءٍ مُضرَّجةٍ،

وتَحْنو فوقنا أُمّاً،

ولكنّ العويلْ ...

يأتي إليها من أقاصينا الشحيحةِ،

يرتمي في حضنها،

يرْتَجُّ في أغصانِها حتى تَميلْ.

فتغيمُ ثانيةً ، وثالثةً،

وتُمطرُ بين أنحاء المَقيلْ.

من أين تُمطرُ ، أو تغيمُ؟

وكيف تَحْنو فوقنا أُمّاً؟

وهل تنْشقُّ من لغةِ العويلْ؟

3.

I attend to the halo of days.
I weep for it and tend to it with verses of sorrow.
Isn't it a halo of fear I have befriended
from day to day?
Here, I don't know how I caught sight of earthen waves
on the blocked roads
or how I glimpsed the longings I had left behind.
Oh, wasteland rippled,
with clouds and despair,
don't you see my face in your vast waving?
Oh, you wasteland that only knows rain by surprise,
rain that beats your stubborn rocks then ceases suddenly.
What do the currents tell you once they rush
like herds of wild horses over your face?
Will you speak?
Or do you prefer to be lulled to sleep
under the currents?
I have come to you not guided but lost.
I found in you my first ribs
and in them the throbbing of rain clouds.
I attend to the halo of days. I weep for it,
as if I have come here in the dream of time
and found my days, their essence flowing
with the tears of Yemen.

Sanaa, Taez (April 20–29, 1992)

. ٣ .

أُعالجُ هالةَ الأيامِ،

أَبْكيها،

أعالجها بآياتٍ من الشجَنِ.

أليستْ هالةَ الخوفِ الذي رافقْتُهُ يوماً إلى يومٍ،

ورافقَني؟

هنا، لم أدرِ كيف لمحتُ أمواجاً مُغفَّرةً،

على الطُرقِ التي انسدَّتْ،

وكيف لمحتُ أشواقي التي فارقْتُها.

يا أيها القفْرُ المُمَوَّجُ،

كيف تأخذني إليكَ على ترانيمِ النحيبْ؟

يا أيها القَفْرُ المُتَوَّجُ،

بالسَّحابِ وبالعذابِ،

ألا ترى وجهي ، تبدَّدَ في تَموُّجِكَ الرحيبْ؟

يا أيها القَفْرُ الذي لا يعرفُ الأمطارَ إلا فجأةً،

فتدقُّ صخرتَه العنيدةَ ، ثم تمضي فجأةً،

ماذا تقولُ لكَ السيولُ إذا جَرَتْ

مثلَ الخيولِ على جبينكَ،

هل تقولْ؟

أم أنتَ تهوى أن تنامَ مُهَدْهَداً تحت السيولْ؟

كأني قد أتيتُ إليكَ لا مُستهْدياً،

بل هائماً،

فوجدتُ عندَكَ أضْلعي الأولى،

وفيها خفْقةُ المُزْنِ.

كأني قد أتيتُ إلى هنا في غفْلةِ الزمنِ.

فوجدتُ أيامي، تقطّرَ ذوْبُها،

في أدْمعِ اليمَنِ.

صنعاء ، تعز (20 . 29 نيسان 1992)

An Evening in Old Sanaa
(To Abdel Aziz al-Maqaleh)

1.

Sanaa has a deep voice,
and we rode the evening
on a high balcony,
nothing above but a few planets,
planets that scattered at the sound of our voices,
at the echoes of what we were about to say.
Were you listening, oh Mosque?
Our words went up
but never came back.
To what then was a listener to listen?
And you, still and silent for hundreds of years,
you see the words we cast into air.
You catch them
and close your impassive eyes.
We sat high above the evening,
on a balcony in the sky,
with our plant awake, visions glowing in it.
We appealed to it to blow the sleep from our blood
and the burning.
We recollect the ruins of the nights
and we restore them
in our warm *maqīl*.
There is a sublime glow to our gathering
and to Sanaa a sonorous voice.

جلسة في صنعاء القديمة
(إلى عبد العزيز المقالح)

.١.

لصنعاءَ صوتٌ عميقٌ.
ونحن اعتلَيْنا المساءَ،
فكانت لنا شرفةٌ عاليهْ.
ليس من فوقها غيرُ بعض الكواكبِ،
تلك التي تتطايرُ من همسنا،
من تردُّد أقوالنا الآتيهْ.
أتسمعُنا أيها الجامعْ؟
يطيرُ الحديثُ بنا،
ثم لا يتساقطُ،
ماذا عساهُ إذن يسمعُ السامعْ؟
غير أنكَ يا أيها القابعُ
من مئات السنين،
تَرى ما نُبدِّدُهُ في المساءِ،
فتحضنُهُ،
ثم تُطْبِقُ أجفانَكَ الساهيهْ.
إذن ، نحن نجلسُ فوق المساءِ،
لنا شرفةٌ في السماءِ،
ونبتتُنا يقظةً، تتوهَّجُ فيها الرؤى
نستجيرُ بها، تُطفئُ النومَ في دمِنا والحريقْ.
نستعيدُ حطامَ الليالي،
نُرمِّمُها في المَقيل الشَّفيقْ.
لجلستنا جذْوةٌ تتسامى،
وصنعاءُ صوتٌ عميقْ.

2.

Sanaa has an ancient face
but it is ours,
when we place our faces in our palms,
we see it and we forbid it to set.
Sanaa has an ancient face,
homes that collapsed into themselves
have struck into the mellowed earth a single root
and stretched, as if they had a single destiny in height.
Homes that tame the mountains,
homes that draw the mountain closer
as if by spell or by calling
homes . . .
Is it fear
that brings them together,
beckoning to each other
in that naked height.
Might they, when crowded,
think themselves safe.
Sanaa has an ancient face
and we who witnessed it,
staring from a balcony in the sky,
were lured by its charm.
We fell together
in sweeping splendor.

Sanaa (5/9/1992)

. ٢ .

لصنعاءَ وجهٌ قديمٌ،

ولكنّه وجهُنا،

حين نمسحُ أوجهَنا بالأكُفّ ، نراهُ،

ونأبى له أن يغيبَ،

لصنعاءَ وجهٌ قديمْ.

... بيوتٌ تداعتْ إلى نفسها،

ضربتْ في الترابِ المُعتَّق جذراً وحيداً لها،

واستطالتْ، كأنّ لها قَدَراً واحداً في العلاءِ،

بيوتٌ، تَراها الجبالُ فتُذْعِنُ،

تهفو إليها الجبالُ المُحيطةُ،

تحسبُها فتنةً أو نداءً،

بيوتٌ ...

تُرى، هل هو الخوفُ ألّفَ ما بينها؟

فتنادتْ إلى بقعةٍ في العراءِ،

عساها إذا ازدحمتْ،

أدركتْ نفسَها في أمانٍ يُقيمْ.

لصنعاءَ وجهٌ قديمْ.

ونحن الذين جلسْنا إليه، نُحدّقُ من شرفةٍ في السماءِ،

تخطّفَنا سِحْرُهُ،

فسقطنا معاً في البهاءِ العميمْ.

صنعاء (1992 . 5 . 9)

Elevation

In every one of my days
I seek shade,
equipped with
my radiance and my retreat
and an introversion toward the creatures of my niche.
Distant and transcendent,
I retire to my days.
I release them
to run free in my private kingdom.
I save them from the crowd that rages outside me.
I retreat to the lands of my kingdom
to save my days,
to release them,
little skies above my corner.

(8/1/1992)

سُمُوّ

إلى رُكْني ...
كما في كلِّ أيامي،
أفيءُ،
وعُدَّتي : أُلَقي، وبُعْدي،
وانطواءٌ لي على الأشياءِ في ركني.
بعيداً، عالياً،
أخلو بأيامي،
أُسرِّحُها، فتعدو حرَّةً في أرض مملكتي،
أُنجّيها من الملأ الذي يهتاجُ خارجَها.
إلى ركني أفيءُ،
لكي أجدِّدَ كلَّ يوم أرضَ مملكتي،
لكي أنجو بأيامي،
وأُطلقَها سماواتٍ على ركني.

(1992 . 8 . 1)

How Long This Day of Mine

1.
Is it not shameful
to outlive one's friends?

2.
Do the dead see, once they have settled
in their death,
what they left behind on the road
where they deserted us?
I wonder,
do they realize the loneliness of the road
once they have left it?
Do they laugh in their death
at our struggling in the strait they have already crossed?
Do they pity us when they look back at where we are?
Do they rejoice in their hearts, that they have made it?
Oh! How beautiful death is,
if the dead look back at the loneliness of the road
once they have settled.

ما أطول يومي هذا

. ١ .

أليس مُخجلاً
أن يعيشَ المرءُ أكثر من أصدقائه؟

. ٢ .

هل يرى المِّيتون إذا ما استقّروا،
هنالك في موتهمْ،
ما تساقطَ منهمْ على الدربِ،
تلك التي خلّفونا عليها؟
تُرى،
هل يرَوْن إلى وحشة الدربِ،
من بعدما خَبَروها؟
وهل يضحكون هنالك في موتهمْ،
من تخبُّطنا في المضيقِ الذي عَبَروهُ؟
تُرى،
يُشْفِقون إذا نظروا حيث نحنُ؟
وهل يفرحون بأنفسهمْ أنْ نَجَوْا؟
آهِ ما أجمل الموتَ،
لو نظرَ المِّيتون إلى وحشةِ الدربِ،
من مُستقَرٍّ لـهمْ.

3.
I look behind me
at each day that passes.
I find it calm, composed
and free,
staring at me with pity,
neither bored nor lonely.
This is how the day passes upon me.
It survives
and hands me coldly to another.
Am I now in another?
This is how the day passes without me
and clears behind me.

4.
Oh! How short life is,
and how long this day of mine!

(2/1/1993)

. ٣ .

كلّما مرَّ يومٌ

نظرْتُ ورائي

فألفيْتُهُ هادئاً، لا يخافُ،

طليقاً،

يُحدِّقُ بي مُشْفِقاً، دونما ضجرٍ،

دونما وحشةٍ،

هكذا ينقضي اليومُ بي.

هُو ينجو،

ويُسْلِمُني في بُرودٍ إلى مثْلِهِ.

هل أنا الآن في مثْلِهِ؟

هكذا ينقضي اليومُ دوني،

ويصفو ورائي.

. ٤ .

ما أقصرَ الحياة،

وما أطولَ يومي هذا!

(1993 . 2 . 1)

There in the Winter

1.
I have closed the doors to women,
the windows once open to desire.
I have left myself only a high balcony
with curtains the colors of fear, longing, and regret.
I have closed the doors to women,
and behind the curtains, I took to a balcony falling away.
A desert rises and stretches over my illusions,
the only pulse remaining that of regret.

2.
Who is the third among us?
You or I or the chill that accompanies us?
Out there in the winter is a wild dove.
It sang on a branch I saw in a dream
and then was lost.
What cold will we face together in the days to come,
when we have no idea, when we are three,
who is the third among us?

(2/11/1993)

هنالك في الشتاء

. ١ .

أقفلتُ أبوابَ النساءِ،
ولم أدَعْ لنوافذِ الشهواتِ إلا شرفةً متعاليهْ.
وستائرَ الخوفِ المُوشّى بالتلهُّفِ والندمْ.
أقفلتُ أبوابَ النساءِ،
فكان لي خلف النوافذ شرفةٌ متهاويهْ.
صحراءُ تنهضُ، أو ترامى فوق أوهامي،
وليس هناك من نبْضٍ
سوى نبْضِ السأمْ.

. ٢ .

مَنْ ثالثٌ فينا؟
أنا أم أنتِ أم بزْدٌ يُصادقُني؟
هنالك في الشتاء يمامةٌ بَرِّيّةٌ،
غنّتْ على غُصنٍ تراءى في منامي .
ثم ضاعتْ ...
أيّ بزْدٍ سوف نلْقاهُ معاً،
فيما سيأتي،
حيث لاندري، ونحن ثلاثةٌ، مَنْ ثالثٌ فينا!

(1993 . 2 . 11)

A Lighthouse for the Drowning

My friends, look closely and you will see how the faces of the land take shape.
You will see a sunny day blemished with prairie flowers as if moonlit.
—Abu Tammam

1.
Our days,
glowing beyond the quivering rooftops,
glitter in the soft rain.
I watch distracted.
I see them, but cannot see myself.
They loom in the distance of my vision.
Can a lighthouse save the drowning?
Peace unto our days as they pulse beyond the curtain.
Peace unto the day that departs,
sunlit or rain-drenched,
carrying in its palms
the clearness of cooling earth.
How can I see from here
the faces of the prairies rise in the open?
I see them emerge like new words.
The sun softly casts its threads about them.
Life flows in them
and flowers rise through them.
The air reveals itself, shadows and light.
Peace unto the day that departs,
sunlit or moonlit,
laughing into a warbling space.

منارةٌ للغريق

يا صاحبيَّ تقصّيا نَظرَيْكُما   تَرَيا وجوهَ الأرض كيف تُصَوَّرُ
تَرَيا نهاراً مُشْمِساً قد شابَه   زهرُ الربى فكأنما هُو مُقْمِرُ
(أبو تَمّام)

. ١ .

هنالك أيامُنا،

تتوهّجُ خلف السطوح التي ارتجفتْ.

تتألّقُ في المطر الناعِمِ.

وأنا أتطلّعُ كالساهِمِ.

فأراها ولا أتبيّنُ نفْسي ...

أراها تَلوحُ بعيداً.

وهل أخذتْ بيد للغريق منارهْ؟

سلاماً لأيامنا وهْي تخفقُ خلف الستارهْ.

سلاماً لذاك النهار الذي يبتعِدْ.

مُمْطراً، مُشْمِساً،

حاملاً بين كفّيْه صحْوَ ثرىً يبترِدْ.

كيف لي أن أرى من مكانيَ هذا وجوهَ الروابي، وقد بزغتْ في العراء؟

أراها وقد فُطِرتْ في العراء كقول جديدٍ،

ومالتْ عليها خيوطٌ من الشمس هامسةٌ،

فترقرق فيها الحياءُ،

وهبَّ لها زَهَرٌ،

فتجلّى الفضاءُ ظلالاً وضوْءاً،

سلاماً لذاك النهار الذي يبتعِدْ.

مُشْمِساً، مُقْمِراً،

ضاحكاً في فضاءٍ غَرِدْ.

How can I see from here
the faces of the prairies emerge in the open?
How can a lighthouse save the drowning?
Our days are there, in the distance,
and here is nothing to bear good news.
My friends, look,
the land is nothing but faces wasting.
Lighthouses wail,
the morning yellow, in which the day has died,
all images on the verge of erasure.
Spring comes.
There is no water clearing into shade,
no flowers rising to eclipse the sun,
so it may float in the prairie sky
like a moon.
This is the wasteland.
My friends, look and you will see
the vast face of death.
Leave me to my solitude,
not the distances ahead.
So I might see myself.
So I might catch a glimpse
of my doubts in a vagrant cloud.

2.
Our days
glow beyond the quivering rooftops,
while here there is nothing
but the wasted face of the land.

(April 1993)

كيف لي أن أرى من مكانيَ هذا

وجوهَ الروابي التي بزغتْ في العراءِ؟

وهل أخذتْ بيدٍ للغريق منارهْ؟

هنالك أيامُنا، فِي البعيدِ،

وليس هنا من يزفُّ بشارهْ.

فيا صاحبيَّ انظُرا،

ليس للأرض إلا وجوهٌ عَفَتْ.

والمناراتُ تُطلقُ ولولةً،

والضحى أصفرٌ، مات فيه النهارُ،

وأوشك يمحو جميع الصُوَرْ.

ويأتي الربيعُ،

فلا الماءُ يصحو ظلالاً،

ولا الزهرُ ينهضُ للشمسِ،

يحجبُ منها ، لتسريَ حالمةً في سماء الربى

كالقمرْ .

هنا القَفْرُ،

يا صاحبيَّ انظُرا،

تَرَيا صفحةً للردى شاسعهْ.

فاتركاني إلى وحدتي ، نحو ذاك البعيدِ،

لكي أتبيَّنَ نفْسي.

لعلّي أرى قَبَساً من ظنونيَ ، في غيمةٍ ضائعهْ.

. ٢ .

هنالك أيامُنا،

تتوهَّجُ خلف السطوحِ التي ارتجفَتْ.

وهنا، ليس للأرضِ إلا وجوهٌ عَفَتْ.

(نيسان 1993)

Forty

If I die, lament me with what I deserve.
    —Tarafa b. al-Abd

1.

Which mourner so I might rest
and accept death descending from the heavens of my fear,
a friend, hesitant as I?
I stand at the verge of forty
releasing my vision, yet it returns.
I see no water
but the dry holes of time,
gaping and black
as graves opening in the distance.
I wonder, where is the mourner so I might rest.
Does a brave hear his own mourning?
Does he walk to death eavesdropping?
How does he walk to death, if the guiding voices have died?
Where have the mourners gone?
Who is a brave? Can he hear the noise around?
Where is the land where I might rest,
where I might steal a moment's pleasure from its refuge?
If it were not for the three pleasures . . .
though three are not mine to claim . . .

الأربعون

إذا متُّ فانعيني بما أنا أهلُهُ ...
(طرفة بن العبد)

. ١ .

أيّ ناعٍ ؟ لكي أطمئنَّ!
وأرتضيَ الموتَ منحدراً من سماواتِ خوفي،
رفيقاً، وقد يتعثَّرُ مثلي.
هي الأربعون،
وقفتُ على شرفةِ الأربعين،
وأطلقتُ عينيَّ ، فارتدَّتا.
لم أرَ الماءَ،
لم أرَ إلا ثقوبَ الزمانِ التي كفَرَتْ بالمياهِ،
تراءتْ لعينيَّ سوداءَ هائلةً،
كالقبورِ التي انبثقتْ في الفضاءِ البعيدِ،
تُرى، أيُّ ناعٍ لكي أطمئنَّ؟
ولكنْ، أيُلْقي الفتى أُذُناً للنَّعيِّ؟
أيمشي إلى الموتِ مُسترقاً سمْعَهُ؟
كيف يمشي إلى موتِه، والمنادون ماتوا؟
أيسمعُ مِنْ حولهِ: مَنْ فتىً؟
أين ولّى المنادون؟
أيّ بلادٍ، لكي أطمئنَّ!
لأُمْضيَ بعض الهنيهات مقتنصاً لذّتي في حماها ...
ولولا ثلاث ...
وليست ثلاثاً، لكي أدَّعيها.

I stand at the verge of forty,
on the peak of years.
I see not the face of life
but the horror of walking to death alone.
I wonder, how does one walk?
Once, looking to the sky in jest,
I saw the shadow of a purebred stallion,
and I thought I had found a way to sleep,
when roaming the earth had worn me out.
I've lost track of the clouds
long ago.
I've lost my stallion and my jest.
I wonder, was I only ever carefree once?
If my god desired, I would have had
another's fortune, another's luck,[6]
but here I am.
This is I.
I stand at the verge of forty.
If my god had desired, he would have granted me a mourner.
How do I proceed now with my lot?
How do I proceed when I haven't yet begun,
when I haven't been carefree even once?

---

[6] The original here quotes a line from Ṭarafa ibn al-'Abd's ode. The line literally translates as:
      If my god desired, I'd be Qays ibn Khalid
      and if my god desired, I'd be 'Amr bin Marthad
The two men referred to in the line are famous leaders of Arab tribes, known for their influence,
fortunes, and noble lineage.

وقفتُ على شرفة الأربعين،

على قمّة العُمْرِ،

لم أرَ وجهَ الحياةِ،

وأبصرتُ هوْلَ المسيرِ إلى الموت وحدي.

تُرى ، كيف يمشي الفتى؟

مَرّةً ، كنتُ ألهو بأن أتطلّعَ نحو الغمامِ،

فأبصرتُ رسْمَ جواد أصيلٍ،

وقلتُ : إذن قد وجدتُ سبيلي إلى النوْمِ،

حين يؤرّقُني السَّيْرُ في الأرضِ،

لكنني من زمان بعيدٍ،

فقَدْتُ الغمامَ،

فقَدْتُ جوادي ، ولَهْوي.

تُرى ، لم يكُنْ لِيَ لَهْوٌ سوى مرّة واحدهْ؟

(ولو شاء ربّي كنتُ قيسَ بن خالد

ولو شاء ربّي كنتُ عمرو بن مَرْثَدِ)

ولكنني ههنا الآنَ،

هذا أنا،

قد وقفتُ على شرفة الأربعين،

ولو شاء ربّي لقدّرَ لي ناعياً.

كيف أمضي بما أنا أهْلٌ لهُ؟

كيف أمضي ولم أبتدئْ؟

لم يكُنْ لِيَ لَهْوٌ ولو مرّةً واحدهْ.

2.

I stand at the verge of forty,
on the peak of years.
I don't see the face of life from this high balcony.
I hear no mourners,
only the moaning of my loneliness.
Have I not stood on this balcony before?
Where are my people and my guides?
Where is the brave?
I see only my shadow fading
into the distant blue.

(May 1993)

. ٢ .

وقفتُ على شرفة الأربعين،

على قمّة العُمرِ،

لم أرَ وجهَ الحياةِ من الشرفة العاليهْ.

أيُّ ناعٍ؟

أليس سوى وحشتي الناعيهْ!

هل وقفتُ على شرفة قَبْلُ،

أين المنادون ، والحَيُّ؟

أين الفتى؟

لا أرى غيرَ ظلّي،

يذوبُ على زُرقةٍ نائيهْ.

(أيار 1993)

Grass

1.
A little grass
growing on oblivious slopes.
It comes back sometimes to flow in my veins
as gentle pain.
It comes as a tender glimpse through the darkness.
It comes soft and bashful,
waving in my mind,
and I remember first steps,
steps that drew small skies to the soil,
when paths led not to terrible peaks
but incremental terrors
to which we surrendered,
terrors that received us
happily.
Then, the darkened skies
became lines we traced,
lines that rose and fell around us.

عُشْب

عُشْبٌ قليلٌ،

نابتٌ فوق السفوح الذاهلاتِ،

يعودُ أحياناً ليسريَ في عُروقي،

مثلَ أوجاعٍ خفيفهْ.

يأتي إليَّ كأنه يثِبُ الظلامَ بلمْحةٍ منهُ رهيفهْ.

يأتي خجولاً ناعماً،

ويموجُ في بالي،

فأذكرُ أوّلَ الخُطُواتِ،

حيث الخَطْوُ يُهْدي للثرى بعضَ السماواتِ الصغيرةِ،

حيث لا تُفْضي الدروبُ إلى ذُرى الأهوالِ،

بل تُفْضي إلى هوْلٍ صغيرٍ،

نرتمي فيهِ، ويلهو بيننا،

فَرِحاً بنا،

فإذا المسافاتُ التي غامتْ

خطوطٌ نحن نرسمُها ، وترقصُ حولنا.

2.

Wet grass
laughing on oblivious slopes.
It comes back sometimes to throb in my veins,
then slides its scars across my hands,
like tattoos to remind me of its fading across the years.
How long will it continue to diminish?
No sooner had it danced in my mind, damp and fresh,
than the slope and sky collapsed
and it was lost.
Yet, I do not know from where
it comes sometimes, to flutter in my veins.

. ٢٠

عُشْبٌ بَليلٌ،

ضاحكٌ فوق السفوحِ الذاهلاتِ،

يعودُ أحياناً ليخفقَ في عُروقي،

ثم يمضي،

تاركاً بعضَ الندوبِ على يَدَيَّ،

كأنّها وشْمٌ،

يُنبِّهُني إلى نأيٍ له عبْرَ السنين،

إلى متى ينأى وينأى؟

لم يكَدْ يختالُ في خَلَدي،

بليلاً، ناضراً،

حتى تهاوتْ أرضُهُ وسماؤهُ،

وأضاعني،

لكنّهُ من حيث لا يدري،

يعودُ إليَّ أحياناً، ليخفقَ في عُروقي.

3.

Greedy grass,
I have only slept in its nest but once.
How can I remember its warmth
after what my memory has endured
of ashes and fire?
How do I find it, when loss has washed the path away
and scattered all beginnings
through time and space?
Was I to awaken to winds
that scattered me in all directions?
I slept not long on that grass,
but I looked to the sky, and it seemed to me to rise and rise.
I lay on my back
and the clouds that lay on the surface of the sky
looked like me.
I lost those clouds.
I slept only awhile on that grass
and then moved on.
Will I ever know its damp scent again?
Grass growing distant,
comes back to me at times, when my days have gone astray.
I wonder, was it the grass that was greedy,
or was it only the burden of years?

(August 1993)

. ٣.

عُشْبٌ بخيلٌ،

لم أنَمْ في مهْدِهِ إلا قليلاً.

كيف أذكُرُ أمْنَهُ،

بعد الذي عَرَفَتْهُ ذاكرتي،

رماداً، أو حرائقَ؟

كيف أُدركُهُ ؟ وقد شطَّتْ بيَ الطُرُقاتُ في تيهٍ،

يُبدِّدُ كلَّ مَهْد في المكانِ،

وكلَّ مَهْد في الزمانِ،

أكان لي أَن أستفيقَ على هبوبٍ،

راح بي في كلِّ صوْبٍ؟

لم أنَمْ إلا قليلاً فوق ذاك العُشْبِ،

لكنّي نظرْتُ إلى السماء، فخِلْتُها تعلو وتعلو ...

كنتُ أستلْقي على ظهْري،

فتُشْبهُني السحاباتُ التي استلْقتْ على كَبِد السماءِ،

فَقَدْتُها ، تلك السحابات القليلهْ.

لم أنَمْ إلا قليلاً فوق ذاك العُشْبِ،

ثم مضيْتُ، لا أدري أأدركُ نفْحةً منه بَليلهْ؟

عُشْبٌ نأى، ويعودُ أحياناً، وقد جمَحَتْ بيَ الأيامُ،

لا أدري أكان هو البخيلُ،

أم السنينُ المُثْخَناتُ هي البخيلهْ؟

(آب 1993)

[73]

Distraction

1.
An evening perched on the scent of jasmine,
perched like a wounded bird shaking nostalgia
from its wings.
I am not here to welcome the evening
but to watch it closely
as I do every day in September.
I yearn for it
and in it find my soul,
perched on the scent of jasmine.
Melancholy evening
in which something flows gently,
flows deep.
Is it yearning?
An irrepressible yearning for all things,
as if I see everything slipping away from me,
as I sit before this evening.
I feel something leave me
yet remain at a distance watching.
Is it poetry?
A spirit that flows deep
and rises effortlessly
to flicker like the passing sky.
Disconsolate evening,
am I not here to embrace it?
To see myself rise little by little into it
and drown in the scent of jasmine.

شُرود

. ١ .

مساءٌ يحُطُّ على عَبَق الياسمينْ.
يحُطُّ كطيْرٍ جريح يُنفِّضُ أجنحةً من حنينْ.
ولستُ هنا كي أُعانِقَهُ،
بل أنا كي أُشاهدَهُ من قريبٍ،
أرى فيه نفْسي تَحُطُّ على عَبَقِ الياسمينْ.
مساءٌ حزينْ.
وشيءٌ يهبُّ خفيفاً،
يهبُّ عميقاً.
أهذا هو الشوقُ؟
شوقٌ طليقٌ إلى كلِّ شيءٍ
كأني أرى ما يفارِقني،
وأنا جالسٌ نحو هذا المساءِ،
يفارِقني كي يشاهدَني من قريبٍ.
أهذا هو الشعرُ؟
روحٌ تهبُّ عميقاً،
وتنسلُّ في خِفّةٍ،
لترفرفَ مثلَ سماءٍ قد انبثقتْ بين حينٍ وحينْ.
مساءٌ حزينْ.
ألستُ هنا كي أُعانِقَهُ؟
كي أرى فيه نفْسي تهبُّ قليلاً قليلاً،
لتغرقَ في عَبَقِ الياسمينْ.

2.

Autumn looms
in the fragrance of September.
Distracted, I am only here this evening
waiting for the wind to scatter me,
waiting for tender extinction.
Does this hypnotic evening know
that when I lose myself to it
I see my soul settle into the incantation of sunset?
I watch it befriend small terrors,
like the wings of fog.
Autumn looms.
September is a gasp of fragrance.
And I am here only in my evening distraction
to exult myself,
to witness it passing like the sky,
tipping the weight of existence,
to find solace within extinction.

(9/10/1993)

. ٢.

خريفٌ يَلوحُ،

وعطرٌ لأيلولَ،

لستُ هنا في شُرودي المسائيِّ إلا

لأشهَدَ سانحةً من هبوبي،

لأشهَدَ سانحةً من فَناءٍ لطيف.

أيعرفُ هذا المساءُ الذي يتخطَّفُني؟

أنني حين أغبطُ نفسي لديْهِ،

أراقبُها وهْي تأنَسُ سحرَ الغيابْ.

أراقبُها وهْي تأمَنُ هوْلاً شفيفاً،

كجُنْح الضبابْ.

خريفٌ يَلوحُ،

وأيلولُ شهْقةُ عطرٍ،

ولستُ هنا في شُرودي المسائيِّ إلا لأغبطَ نفْسي،

لأشهَدَها وهْي تخطرُ مثلَ الهواءْ.

تُحرّكُ ثِقْلَ الوجودِ،

وتتأنَسُ معنى الفَناءْ.

(1993 . 9 . 10)

Heavy Essence

I am not the first whose shirt is filled with the musk of pride
while his pocket is riddled with holes.
The aspirations of men are grand.
They continue to expand as time shrinks.
  —Al-Sharīf al-Radī

1.

A spirit concealed within my shirt
directs me.
Whenever it urges me on, I pause
and when it restrains me, I charge.
But if I were to see my path
or my stumbling
it would envelope me, swelling,
welcoming as an embrace.
It is my light and my labyrinth,
my awareness and enticement,
safety and fear,
but it always receives me like a stronghold.
I exult in the height and the view.
It has always been my friend,
hidden within my array.

عَبَق

ما كنتُ أوّلَ مِنْ جثا بقميصِهِ   عَبَقُ الفَخارِ وجيْبُهُ مخروقُ
كثُرَت أمانيُّ الرجالِ ولم تزلْ   مُتوسِّعاتٍ والزمانُ يضيقُ

(الشريف الرضي)

١٠.

عَبَقٌ كامنٌ في قميصي،

يُوجِّهُني.

كلَّما حثَّني أتلجلجُ،

أو ردَّني أتحفَّزُ،

لكنَّني إذْ أرى وُجْهتي،

أو أرى عثْرتي،

يتخطَّفُني خافقاً في قميصي،

رحيباً كحِضْنٍ.

هو الضوءُ لي والمتاهةُ،

والرُشْدُ والغيُّ،

والأمنُ والخوفُ،

لكنّه دائماً يتلقَّفُني مثلَ حصْنٍ،

فآنَسُ بي عالياً، مُشْرِفاً،

هو يَرْبي،

لقد كان لي منذ كنتُ،

وما زال مُسْتخْفياً في قميصي.

2.

A spirit lingers beneath my shirt,
buried like a secret.
It teaches me how to survive
when time is ruled
by the whims of humans.
It teaches me how to see
when every direction is clouded by them.
It teaches me to despair in all things,
to love all things,
and leaves me lost between the two.
I wander,
and it blossoms in the darkness of my soul.

3.

There is a spirit within my shirt,
hidden,
because space is so small
and some hopes go on forever.

(11/10/1993)

. ٢ .

عَبَقٌ كامنٌ في قميصي،

دفينٌ كسرٍّ.

يُعلِّمُني كيف أنجو،

إذا حكَمَتْ في الزمانِ صغائرُ أهلِ الزمانِ،

يُعلِّمُني كيف أصفو،

إذا عكَّرَ الناسُ حولي جميعَ الجهاتِ،

يُعلِّمُني اليأسَ من كلِّ شيءٍ،

ويتركُني هائماً بين حبٍّ ويأسٍ.

أهيمُ،

فتورقُ أغصائهُ في غَيابة نفْسي.

. ٣ .

عَبَقٌ كامنٌ في قميصي،

خبيءٌ،

لأنَّ الفضاءَ قليلُ.

وبعض الأماني طويلٌ ... طويلُ.

(1993 . 11 . 10)

Day

The dearest thing to me was the garden in prayer,
as it dried morning tears.
Around me the remains of the night before:
cigarette ashes
and the lingering dark in the bottom of a glass.
These obsessions, perched on the fading papers
on the table, have for long now shared my nights.
They have even begun to share my trembling
when despised by a distant thought.
The closest thing to me was the prayer of the garden,
but, now, where will you drag me, oh day?
Shall I rise to witness your death over the wild lands?
Shall I set out towards you?
You, heavy and weary like me.
I only see you reveal our flaws.
Why do you tempt me to you every day?
You motion to me and we both rise from our living wakes,
from the insomnia of the night before.
We both remain staring into a darkness that doesn't lend the
        drowning a hand,
each dissipating into an outward gaze.
We remain like that until I see you rise thread by thread from your
        distractions.
Why then do you tempt me to walk toward you?
Won't you be so kind as to leave without me one day,
to trace your frail threads in all directions.
Walk away and leave me,
so I might sleep through the morning
on a sheet of garden prayers,
among the remains of the night before.

(2/2/1994)

نَهار

كان أقربَ شيءٍ إليَّ صلاةُ الحديقةِ،
وهْي تُكفكفُ دمعَ الصباحِ،
وحولي بقايا السهادِ من الليلةِ الماضيةْ:
رمادُ السجائرِ،
والكأسُ ، في قعْرِها ظلمةٌ باقيةْ.
وهواجسُ حطَّتْ على ورقٍ باهتٍ،
فوق طاولةٍ شاركتْني الجلوسَ إلى الليل منذ زمان طويلٍ،
وباتتْ تشاركُني رجفتي ، حين تُزْري بنا فكرةٌ نائيةْ.
كان أقربَ شيءٍ إليَّ صلاةُ الحديقةِ،
لكنْ،
إلى أين سوف تُجرجرُ بي أيُّها النهارْ؟
أأنهضُ بعد قليلٍ لأشهَدَ موتَكَ فوق القِفارْ؟
أمضي إليكَ؟
وأنتَ الذي تتثاقلُ مثلي،
ولستُ أراكَ تُضيءُ سوى عثْرةٍ لكَ ... أو لي.
لماذا تُغرِّرُ بي كلَّ يومٍ؟
فتومئُ لي كي أسيرَ إليكَ،
ونحن كلانا أتيْنا من السُّهْدِ، من أرَقِ الليلةِ الماضيةْ.
كلانا ظَلَلْنا نُحدِّقُ في ظلمةٍ لا تَمَدُّ يداً للغريقِ،
ظَلَلْنا نُحدِّقُ كلٌّ إلى جهة لا تَبادلُه نظرةً،
وظَلَلْنا كذلك حتى رأيتُكَ تبزغُ من تَرَّهاتكَ خيطاً فخيطاً.
لماذا تُراودُني الآن حتى أسيرَ إليكَ؟
ألا تتكرَّمُ يوماً ؟ فتمضي بدوني،
لترسمَ بين الجهاتِ أحابيلَكَ الواهيةْ.
تولَّ ودعْني،
لعلّي أنامُ الصباحَ على صفحةٍ من صلاةِ الحديقةِ،
بين بقايا السهادِ مِن الليلة الماضيةْ.

(1994 . 2 . 2)

Night

The dearest thing to me was the garden in prayer,
as it bid the setting sun farewell.
It slid out of one dress and into another,
a fragrance quivering like visions in its robes.
And I,
did I witness or disintegrate?
I cannot say.
Visions are but trances.
I feel myself slacken bit by bit.
Come, then, oh night.
Soon we will begin our ritual.
You will take me under your robes in diffidence,
and you will be as tender as you can,
but sleep will soon defeat you.
You will abandon the temptations I have set for you:
a book, a glass, a pack of cigarettes.
You will despair of me at midnight,
throwing yourself into a fatigue of ash,
and I will remain behind with my insomnia.

(2/21/1994)

لَيْل

كان أقربَ شيءٍ إليَّ صلاةُ الحديقةِ،
وهْي تُودِّعُ شمسَ المغيبِ،
فتخلعُ ثوباً، وتلبسُ ثوباً،
ويختلجُ العطرُ مثلَ الرؤى بين أثوابِها.
وأنا ... يا تُرى،
أترقَّبُ أم أتناثرُ؟
لستُ أفرِّقُ،
لكنني، والرؤى غفلةٌ، أتثاقلُ شيئاً فشيئاً.
تعالَ إذن أيُّها الليلُ،
عمّا قليل سيبدأُ ما بيننا سَمَرٌ يتكرَّرُ في كلِّ يومٍ،
ستأخذُني تحت ثوبكَ في خَفَرٍ،
وسترفقُ بي ما استطعْتَ،
ولكنْ، سيأخُذُ منكَ النعاسُ سريعاً،
ستعزفُ عمّا تدبَّرْتُهُ لكَ من مُغْرَياتٍ:
كتابٍ، وكأسٍ، وعلبة تبْغٍ ...
ستيأسُ مني إذا ما انتصفْتَ،
وتُلْقي بنفسِكَ في وهَنٍ كالرمادْ.
... وأبقى أنا للسهادْ.

(1994 . 2 . 21)

Light Pulse

1.

A light pulse in the trees,
and a stiffness on the couch where I sit
looking through the glass,
forgetting the point of seeing.
My eyes glass behind glass,
and my fingers the glow of a burning light
that traveled through my hands and left a throbbing,
an earthy glimmer, and light pains.
My gaze breaks short of the outside that eyes me
with a faint smile.
A weary pulse in the trees.
I am weary against it,
listening to the pulse in my veins race or grow faint.
I cannot tell, except that when I listen to it,
I feel the directions whirl around me.
I see the balconies slant, the windows deprived of eyelids.
The clouds come from afar to sit with me and fill my room with
        their heavy scent.
To whom do I call out?

نبْضٌ خفيف

. ١ .

نبْضٌ خفيفٌ في الشجرْ.
وتصلُّبٌ فوق الأريكة حيث أجلسُ،
ناظراً عبْرَ الزجاج،
وناسياً معنى النظَرْ.
عينايَ خلف زجاج نافذتي زجاجْ.
وأصابعي وهْجُ احتراقاتٍ خفيفهْ،
عَبَرَتْ يديَّ وخلَّفتْ بعضَ اختلاجْ،
ألَقاً ترابياً، وأوجاعاً طفيفهْ.
عينايَ تقتربان من نفسي التي وهَنَتْ،
وتنكسران دون الخارج المُزْبَدِّ، يرمقُني،
ويمنحُني ابتساماً باهتاً.
نبْضٌ كليلٌ في الشجرْ.
وأنا الكليلُ أمامهُ،
أُصغي إلى نبْضٍ تسارعَ في عُروقي، أو تبدَّدَ،
لستُ أدري، غيرَ أني حين أسمعُهُ، تدورُ بيَ النواحي،
أُبصرُ الشرفاتِ قد مالتْ، وأسْبَلَت النوافذُ بعض أجفان لها،
وأتتْ غيومٌ من بعيدٍ كي تُجالسَني، وتملأُ غرفتي عَبَقاً ثقيلاً،
من أُنادي؟

Where is that enchanting light that summoned me,
the faint pulse in the trees?
My eyes approach my frail being
and break against my fears.
Rise then you trees that have slumbered for ages in my veins.
You are I,
so rise.
There's nothing else I can call upon.
The whole universe has grown pale.
So come you trees
that are within me.
Your day has come. You have spent an age awaiting.

2.
My time is an arc
tied by a thread
to the arc of the sky.
When my days tighten around me,
the sky opens and embraces me.
They are two arcs bound
by a single thread of hope.

(1/24/1994)

أين ولّى ذلك الضوءُ الخرافيُّ الذي
قد لاح لي نبْضاً خفيفاً في الشجرْ؟
عينايَ تقتربان من نفْسي التي وهَنَتْ،
وتنكسران قرب مخاوفي.
إنهضْ إذن يا أيها الشجرُ الذي
قد نِمْتَ دهْراً في عُروقي،
أنتَ ذُخْري،
فاسْتَفِقْ،
لا شيءَ حولي أستعينُ بهِ،
قد اصفرَّ الفضاءُ بأسْرهِ،
فتعالَ يا هذا الشجرْ.
أنتَ الذي في داخلي،
قد جاء يومُكَ،
بعدما أمْضَيْتَ دهراً تنتظِرْ.

. ٢ .

زمني له قوْسٌ،
وقوْسٌ للسماءْ.
شُدّا بخيْطٍ،
كلّما ضاقتْ بيَ الأعوامُ،
آنَسْتُ السماءَ تضُمُّني... وتَضُمُّني.
قوْسان بينهما إذن خيْطُ الرجاءْ.

(1994 . 1 . 24)

Land

The noble man does not alight upon an easy land,
and flight will not avail the lowly.
—al-Hārīth b. Ḥilliza

1.
These words,
I saw them quickly cross the field
and the space awakened.
Words,
when they pass the frail trees,
the trees become heavy with tears.
Words,
they are the lost homeland
and we, the rubble and remains.

2.
Homeland
has become desolate with us.
We set out before light
but found no way.
Homeland,
we speak it and we name it,
and the words and names weep.
Homeland
spins in a limp age
deafened by echoes.
How did time become so small?
Its yellow shadows despise us.
There's nothing but astonishment
in every direction,
and if you walk, the roads deceive.

بلاد

لا يُقيمُ العزيزُ في البلد السهْلِ   ولا ينفعُ الذليلَ النَّجاءُ
(من معلقة الحارثَ بن حلّزة)

. ١ .

كلماتٌ،
رأيتُها تعبُرُ السهْلَ سريعاً،
فيسْتفيقُ الفضاءُ.
كلماتٌ،
تَمرُّ بالشجر الواهي مروراً،
فيعتريه بكاءُ.
كلماتٌ،
هي البلادُ التي ضاعتْ،
ونحن الفلولُ والأشلاءُ.

. ٢ .

يا بلاداً،
أمستْ بنا مُقْفِراتٍ،
وغَدَوْنا،
فما هناك نَجاءُ.
يا بلاداً،
نقولُها ونُسمّيها،
فتبكي الأقوالُ والأسماءُ.
يا بلاداً،
تدوخُ في الزمنِ الرَّخْوِ،
وتُودي بسمْعِها الأصداءُ.
كيف أضحى الزمانُ فينا قليلاً؟
تزدرينا ظلالُهُ الصفراءُ.
ليس إلا الذهولُ،
في كلِّ صوْبٍ،
وإذا سِرْتَ، فالدروبُ رياءُ.

[91]

3.
Words,
we live in,
when there's nowhere to settle
and the directions themselves close down.
Words,
they are home,
the land and the sky to us
and everything between.

(1/8/1995)

. ٣.
كلماتٌ،
نُقيمُ فيها،
إذا عزَّ مقامٌ،
وأطْبَقَتْ أرجاءُ.
كلماتٌ،
هي الديارُ،
هي الأرضُ لنا، والسماءُ، والأشياءُ.

(1995 . 1 . 8)

Stars

1.
We fear life,
but we do not die of fear.

2.
Our stars are unlike stars.
They do not shine in nearby skies.
Night is not like night when it holds them,
and the clouds that approach them
are summer clouds,
clouds of lightning
that forever approach us and our stars
but are unlike clouds.
They are stars
we haven't seen yet.
They have settled into the words we haven't said,
which is why they loom over us every day.
They loom every night
and breathe vision into us like a haze.
Stars of ours that do not sleep,
aimlessly wandering the night sky.
Stars, our words in a day that will never come.

نجومٌ لنا لم تُضِىْ

. ١ .

نخافُ الحياةَ،
ولكننا لا نموتُ من الخوفْ.

. ٢ .

نجومٌ لنا،
لم تُضِىْ في السماءِ القريبةِ،
ليستْ كمثل النجومِ.
ولا الليلُ كالليل حين يُعانقُها،
والغيومُ التي تتقرَّبُ منها،
سحاباتُ صيفٍ،
سحاباتُ بَرْقٍ،
تُديمُ التقرُّبَ منها، ومنّا.
وليستْ كمثل الغيومِ.
نجومٌ لنا،
لانراها،
ولكنّها سَكَنَتْ في الكلامِ الذي لم نقُلْهُ،
لهذا ، تراودُنا كلَّ يومٍ،
تراودُنا كلَّ ليْلٍ،
وتبعثُ فينا رؤىً كالسديمِ.
نجومٌ لنا ... لا تنامُ.
يهيمُ بها الليْلُ والغيْمُ،
وهْي لنا في غدٍ ليس يأتي كلامُ.

3.
Stars of ours,
they do not shine in nearby skies
but put themselves out beyond the heavens.
They blew out in our sockets.
They were only secrets
that elevated us.
They were only secrets
settled under the dark,
throbbing between our fingers.
Stars of ours
that did not shine in the shroud of night,
but we took joy in them
when the night was a gloom all around us.

4.
To our children, we write:
We are not your lighthouse.
Do not follow the path we light,
but be your own secrets.

(February 1995)

. ٣.

نجومٌ لنا،

لم تُضِئْ في السماءِ القريبةِ،

لكنها بَذَلَتْ نفْسَها ما وراء السماواتِ،

وانطفأتْ ... في محاجرِنا.

لم تكُنْ غيرَ أسرارِنا،

وهْي تعلو بنا ...

لم تكُنْ غيرَ أسرارِنا،

وهْي تهبطُ تحت الظلامِ،

لتخفقَ بين أصابعِنا ...

نجومٌ لنا ، لم تُضِئْ في الليالي التي اكتنفتْنا.

ولكنْ نَعِمْنا بِها ، والليالي دياجيرُ من حولنا.

. ٤.

كتبْنا لأبنائنا: نحن لسنا منائِرَكُمْ

لا تكونوا خُطانا، وكونوا سرائِرَكُمْ.

(شباط 1995)

Bird

1.
The heart lies,
and drops in the pit of the body
heavy beats.
The heart lies,
and sends to the far limbs lightning
and night-long shivers.

2.
The heart plays, it does not lie.
It plays, drumming among lowly organs.

3.
It is the heart then,
the bird of this body.
In its pit, it plays.
In its pit, it strives.
It forever flies wingless within its thoracic cage.
Wrestling with echoes,
choking sometimes,
shy as shy words,
noble as noble words.

4.
It is the heart.
It will fall asleep tomorrow.
Then, would the bird break free from the pit of this body,
a bird promised beyond these arid skies,
slaking the skies?

(April 1995)

عصفور

. ١ .

يكذبُ القلبُ،
فتهْوي منه في حفرةِ هذا الجسمِ دقّاتٌ ثقيلهْ.
يكذبُ القلبُ،
فيسْري منه في الأطرافِ بَرْقٌ،
وارتعاشاتٌ طويلهْ.

. ٢ .

يلعبُ القلبُ ... ولا يكذبُ،
يلهو ... خافقاً ما بين أعضاءٍ ذليلهْ.

. ٣ .

إنه القلبُ إذن،
عصفورُ هذا الجسمِ،
في حفرتهِ يعبثُ،
في حفرتهِ يخبطُ،
يبقى طائراً في قفص الصدرِ بلا أجنحةٍ،
مُرْتطماً فيه بأصداءٍ لهُ،
مُحْتبساً بعضَ اختناقاتٍ،
خجولاً مثلَ أقوالٍ خجولهْ.
ونبيلاً مثلَ أسرارٍ نبيلهْ.

. ٤ .

إنه القلبُ ...سيغفو في غدٍ ...
إذّاك هل يُفلتُ من حفرةِ هذا الجسمِ عصفورٌ،
له خلف السماواتِ التي جفّتْ،
سماواتٌ ظليلهْ؟

(نيسان 1995)

[99]

My Evening There

1.
My evening there is the evening of trees,
sullen trees waiting for dark,
staring in silence,
raising their branches;
arms that rise from a wreck,
calling for help, without hope, without words.

2.
My evening there is the evening of trees
frightened before dark,
their branches are their fear
and the air that turns within them dumb.
The space is heavy, and they succumb.

3.
My evening there is a mirage in the treetops.
When it perches on them, I feel it, though I cannot see.
It shines within me.
I do not see it, but it fills me with bliss.
How does the mirage of trees come to me?
How does it touch me?
How does it shine within?
I don't see it, but filled with bliss it scatters me
over the treetops.
How does the evening come to me as a friend
yet remain distant and strange?
How can a mirage come so close?

مسائي هناك

.١.

مسائي هناك مساءُ الشجيْراتِ،
واجمةً في انتظارِ الظلامْ.
تُحدِّقُ في الصمتِ،
ترفعُ أغصانُها أذْرُعاً نبتَتْ في حُطامْ.
تستغيثُ بلا أملٍ ... أو كلامْ.

.٢.

مسائي هناك مساءُ الشجيْراتِ،
وهْي تخافُ قُبيْلَ الظلامِ،
وأغصانُها خوفُها.
والهواءُ الذي يتلوّى بداخلها أبْكَمُ.
والفضاءُ ثقيلٌ ، فتسْتَسْلِمُ.

.٣.

مسائي هناك سرابٌ بأعلى الشجيْراتِ،
حين يحُطُّ عليها أُحِسُّ بهِ، لا أراهُ،
ويلمعُ في داخلي.
لا أراهُ ، ولكنني أحتويهِ،
ويملؤني نعْمةً،
كيف يأتي إليَّ سرابُ الشجيْراتِ؟
كيف يُلامسُني؟
كيف يلمعُ في داخلي؟
لا أراهُ،
ولكنني أتبدَّدُ فوق الذُّرى،
حين يملؤني نعْمةً.
كيف يأتي المساءُ إليَّ خليلاً،
ويبقى لديَّ خجولاً غريبا.
كيف يُمسي السرابُ هناك قريباً قريبا.

4.

My evening there is a spell,
a fading,
a shimmering
and an awakening against the drowsiness of the garden,
an illusion,
and a longing toward all that lures me.
Everything here indulges me
as it dwindles bit by bit,
until it bashfully emerges from itself
and settles into a darkness of trees.

(9/5/1995)

. ٤ .

مسائي هناك انخطافٌ، تلاشٍ،
هبوبٌ عميقٌ،
وصحْوٌ أمام نُعاس الحديقةِ،
وهْمٌ، وشوقٌ إلى كلِّ ما يتخطَّفُني ...
كلُّ شيءٍ هناك يُلاطِفُني،
وهْو يخبو قليلاً قليلاً،
ليخرجَ من نفْسِهِ في خَفَرْ.
ويغربَ مُنْكَمِشاً في ظلام ِ الشجرْ.

(1995 . 9 . 5)

The Slanted Balcony

When I open my eyes, I open them unto many but see none.
—Duʿbul al-Khuzāʿī

1.
My vision is level
yet these trees slant
and the people
slant,
and there is nothing where I sit but boredom
and a little dizziness to distract me.
Though I'm dizzy my gaze doesn't slant.
It grows tired yet remains steady
in its stupefaction. Thus I'm left to despair in this heavy time.

الشُّرفةُ المائلة

إني لأفتحُ عيني حين أفتحُها   على كثيرٍ ولكنْ لا أرى أحدا
(دعبل الخزاعي)

. ١.

نظرتي لا تميلُ،

ولكنّ هذا الشجرَ

مائلٌ،

والبشَرْ

مائلونَ،

وليس هنا حيث أجلسُ غيرُ الضجَرْ

ودُوارٌ خفيفٌ يُشتِّتُني ...

يعتريني الدُّوارُ، ولكنّ لي نظرةً لا تميلْ.

تكِلُ، ولكنّها لا تميلْ.

تضيعُ، وتتركني يائساً في الزمانِ الثقيلْ.

2.

Though my vision does not slant
this horizon betrays me.
It neither relents nor straightens
but evades me.
All I see is vast emptiness.
It dodges my gaze
and guards like a watchman.
It oscillates in my eyes.
I say: the horizon is a straw,
and I take refuge in myself.
I indulge around me stars that have faded
and stars that soon will fade.
I say: the horizon is dark,
and on my balcony I drink to the despairing moon.
I speak only my disappointment
and cast an unerring gaze upon the open.

3.

My gaze does not slant,
if even I were looking from a slanted balcony.
My gaze does not break,
but brings an immense desolation.

(9/10/1995)

. ٢ .

نظرتي لا تميلُ،

وهذا المدى جاحدٌ،

لا يرقُّ ولا يستقيمُ،

يُراوغُني،

لا يُقابلُني منه غيرُ خواءٍ رحيبْ.

يحاذرُ هذا المدى نظرتي،

يترصَّدُها كالرقيبْ.

يتأرجحُ في ناظريَّ،

أقولُ: المدى قشَّةٌ،

وألوذُ بنفْسي.

أقولُ: المدى جاحدٌ،

وألاطفُ حولي نجوماً خَبَتْ ونجوماً ستخبو .

أقولُ: المدى قاتمٌ،

وأُنادمُ في شرفتي قمراً يائساً ...

لا أقولُ سوى خيْبتي،

حين أُرسلُ عبْرَ المدى نظرةً لا تَخيبْ.

. ٣ .

نظرتي لا تميلُ،

وإنْ كنتُ أنظرُ من شرفة مائلهْ.

نظرتي لا تميلُ،

لذا، تجلبُ الوحشةَ الهائلهْ.

(1995 . 9 . 10)

The Sky That Denied Me

The sky that sheltered me by morning
abandoned me by night.
I begged, but it would not return.
So I sat on a balcony in fading shades of sunset.
And the sky stayed away.
But I could feel it still.
I reached beyond myself,
beyond my senses to embrace it,
after it left me alone in dying light.

(1/5/1996)

السماءُ التي أنكرتْني

السماءُ التي ظلَّلَتْني صباحاً،
شعرتُ بِها في المساءِ، وقد أنكرتْني.
وقفتُ إليها، فلم تقتربْ.
وجلستُ إليها على شرفةٍ من ظلال المغيبِ،
فلم تقتربْ.
غير أني شعرتُ بِها،
فذهبتُ إليها بعيداً بعيدا.
ورحتُ أُعانقُها،
بعدما خلّفتْني على شرفةٍ من ظلال المغيب وحيدا.

(1996 . 1 . 5)

Winter's Words

When winter pays a visit, it finds me away.
I'm always late for our dates.
It is time, and yet where am I?
Winter and I . . .
It comes and I miss it.
I know it only by its calling.
Every time it comes, it leaves a couple words,
drizzle, blame, sometimes a promise.
I learn what I can, without coming to tears.
For I have come to know a few words of winter.

(1/8/1996)

كلامُ الشتاء

أنا والشتاءُ ...
إذا جاء لم يُلْقَني،
أتأخَّرُ عن موعد بيننا قد عقدْناهُ يوما.
يحينُ ، ولكنني أتأخَّرُ دوْما.
أنا والشتاءُ ...
يجيءُ،
وأُخطئهُ،
لستُ أدركُ إلا تحيّاتِهِ،
فهُو يتركُ لي كلّما جاء بعض كلامٍ،
رذاذاً،
ولوْماً،
وعهْداً جديداً،
ألملمُ ما أستطيعُ، وأخشى البكاءْ.
فإني تعلّمْتُ بعض كلام الشتاءْ.

(1996 . 1 . 8)

[111]

Birds of Regret

Am I not he who is visited from time to time
by birds with crippled wings?
Am I not he who takes refuge in illusions
when the birds of regret descend?
He who stares long enough
he finds even illusions evasive,
illusions like illness in his yellow eyes?
Am I not he . . .
who goes back to himself
and falls in hope of sleep
before the birds of regret descend?

(1/9/1996)

طُيورُ الندم

ألستُ أنا ... من تُعاودُهُ بين حين وحين
طُيورٌ بأجنحة واهيةْ؟
ألستُ أنا ... مَن يلوذُ بأوهامِهِ النائيةْ ...
كلّما عاودتْهُ طُيورُ الندمْ؟
فينأى قليلاً، يُطالعُ أوهامَهُ غيرَ عابئةٍ،
تتراءى لعيْنيْه مثلَ السَّقَمْ.
ألستُ أنا ... من يعودُ إلى نفْسِهِ،
وينامُ على أمَل أنْ ينامَ،
فتأتي إليه طُيورُ النَّدَمْ؟!

(9 . 1 . 1996)

[113]

Smoke
(To Beirut)

1.
I exhale
and see through smoke
the faces of the city.
When the faces fade,
do I resurrect them,
do I blow them out into a desolate sky,
or is it a restless sky buried in my lungs?

2.
The faces of the city have faded.
For a while they taunted me,
and I fell for it every time.
I smoke,
but in vain discern a face,
in vain discern a face, even if cruel,
like the face the city turned to me
when first I came to her,
hoping for a little charm beyond the cruelty,
an ensnaring charm.
In vain, I recall my first tryst with this city.
How mysterious it was
and how I delighted in that alluring mystery
like a tender love
soon lost.
Time eventually dressed it in shabby clothes.

دخان

(إلى بيروت)

. ١ .

أُدخِّنُ،

حتى أرى من خلال الدخان وجوهَ المدينةْ.

وجوهُ المدينة غارتْ،

أَلبعثُها في دخاني؟

وأنفثُها في السماء التي أَقْفَرَتْ؟

أم تُراني أُدغدغُ في رئتيَّ سماءً دفينةْ؟

. ٢ .

وجوهُ المدينة غارتْ،

وكانت زماناً تراوغُني،

وأنا كنتُ أهوي بها كلّما راوغتْني.

أُدخِّنُ،

لكنني عَبَثاً أتبيَّنُ وجهاً لها،

عَبَثاً أَتبيّنُ وجهاً، ولو قاسياً،

مثلَ ذاك الذي واجهتْني بهِ،

عندما جئتُها أَتوسّمُ خلف القساوة سحراً، تخطَّفني بَرْقُهُ،

عَبَثاً أَستعيدُ لقائي بهذي المدينةِ،

كمْ كان مُلتبِساً،

كم فرحْتُ بذاك الغموض الذي شدَّني أوّلاً،

شدَّني مثلَ حُبّ طريٍّ،

وسرعانَ ما ضاعَ،

جرَّ عليه الزمانُ الذي مرَّ أردائَهُ الكالحاتِ،

I smoke,
and the smoke teases me.
It waves to me, weary,
as the city grows sullen and black.
The mystery that first drew me does not return.
Why do I take refuge in this smoke?
Might I relight what time has blown out?

3.
The faces of the city fade.
Nothing is left but the windows of withered cafes
and an empty sky.
Behind the glass I blow my smoke at the sky
and I see the face of sunset in the streets.
Everything has passed on and settled in the dark,
and the directions have all dispersed.
In this smoke I see only the dying of directions.
I smoke so I may not see.
There is nothing but the silence.
Nothing rises, not even words.
Everything has already passed on and settled in the dark.

(February 1996)

أُدخِّنُ،
يهزأُ مني دخاني،
يُلوِّحُ لي خائراً،
والمدينةُ تَسْودُّ واجمةً،
والغموضُ الذي شدَّني أوّلاً لا يعودُ،
لماذا ألوذُ بهذا الدخانْ؟
أيُرْجِعُ ما أطفأتْهُ صروفُ الزمانْ؟

．٣．

وجوهُ المدينة غارتْ،
ولم يبْقَ إلا زجاجُ المقاهي التي ذبلتْ،
والسماءُ التي أقْفَرتْ.
وأنا من وراء الزجاج أدخِّنُ نحو السماءِ،
وألمحُ عبْرَ الشوارع وجْهَ الغروبِ،
مضى كلُّ شيءٍ إلى مُسْتَقَرٍّ له مظلمٍ،
والجهاتُ اضْمَحَلَّتْ،
ولستُ أرى في دخاني إذنْ غيرَ موتِ الجهاتِ،
أُدخِّنُ كي لا أرى،
ليس غيرُ الوجومِ،
أُدخِّنُ،
لا شيءَ ينهضُ ... حتى الكلامْ.
مضى كلُّ شيءٍ إلى مُسْتَقَرٍّ له في الظلامْ.

(شباط 1996)

Dying Directions

1.

The directions converge here from every side
and they die
like a strange sky revealed.
The directions die here
in this place that darkens
like the face of prey.

2.

I have lost my passions
sitting here watching.
I rise from time to time
and everything shrinks in my eyes.
Why do I keep watch?
What will I have accomplished when wandering has worn me out
and the pain in my back grows?
I lost my bewilderment
sitting here longing for illusions.
For what was I preparing?
And how do I face this darkness that approaches?

جهاتٌ تموت

‏. ١ .

تموتُ الجهاتُ هنا،
فوق هذا المكان الذي أقبلَتْ فيه من قبْلُ،
وانكشفتْ كسماءٍ فريدهْ.
تموتُ الجهاتُ هنا،
فوق هذا المكان الذي يكْفَهِرُّ كوجه الطريدهْ.

‏. ٢ .

أضعْتُ جموحي هنا،
وجلستُ أراقبُ،
أُصلحُ من جلستي بين حين وحينٍ،
ويصغُرُ في نَظَري كلُّ شيءٍ.
لماذا أراقبُ؟
ماذا عسايَ سأُصلحُ حين تضيعُ غداً جلستي،
ويكِلُّ شرودي،
وتشتدُ آلامُ ظَهْري؟
أضعْتُ هنا حيْرتي،
وجلستُ أُقاسي افتقاراً إلى الوهمِ،
ماذا أعدُّ؟
وكيف أُواجهُ هذا الظلامَ الذي يتقدَّمُ نحوي؟

[119]

From this height, I've learned the meaning of falling.
I've watched scenes collapse.
They noticed my amazement as they fell, and they laughed.
I wonder, what heritage can straighten my figure?
What glorious past?
This place is prepared to receive, day after day,
any form of collapse that will scatter my illusions
and concentrate the pain in my back.
Here, in this place, I have learned what it is to fall.
I have become addicted to loving this place
that destroyed me once then twice then three times.
What love is this that suffocates me?
What death?
I tire of loving to death
and dying of love.
I destroy myself
watching over this place.
I sit up as straight as I can
and I become content,
as content as I am with the pain in my back.

هنا فوق هذا المكانِ تعلّمتُ معنى السقوطِ،
رأيْتُ المَشاهدَ تهْوي،
شهدْتُ المَشاهدَ من كلِّ نوعٍ،
وكانت ترى دهشتي وهْي تهْوي،
فتهزأ مني.
تُرى أيُّ إرْثٍ سيُصلحُ من جلستي؟
أيُّ إرْثٍ؟
وهذا المكانُ مُعَدٌّ لكي يتلقَّفَ يوماً فيوماً
أفانينَ هذا السقوط الذي يتولّى بوهْمي،
ويُخْصِبُ آلامَ ظَهْري.
هنا فوق هذا المكانِ تعلّمْتُ معنى السقوطِ،
وأدمنْتُ حُبَّ المكانِ الذي ...
والمكان الذي ...
والمكانِ الذي هدّني مرّةً، مرّتيْن، ثلاثاً ...
تُرى أيُّ حُبّ يسدُّ عليَّ الفضاءَ؟
تُرى أيُّ موتٍ؟
سئمْتُ من الحُبِّ موتاً،
من الموتِ حُبّاً.
أراقبُ هذا المكانَ، فأُتلِفُ نفْسي،
وأُصلحُ من جلستي ما استطعْتُ،
وأرضى،
كما قد رضيتُ بآلامِ ظَهْري.

3.

Here in this place the directions die.

Everything shuts down, even the plants.

All I have are longings,

even a yearning for the shivers of a winter whose lies exhausted me.

I trust nothing but my despair.

I see it everywhere, yellow, filling the streets, between the homes,

in the trees.

Where is the wilderness?

Where are the vast tracts of land?

The mountains? The floating peaks?

I only believe my shrinking and my despair.

The winter, whose lies once wearied me, is now dead.

Here vanities dance.

Here, in this darkening place, the directions lie down and die.

Everything collapses . . . even the plants.

(March 1996)

. ٣ .

هنا فوق هذا المكانِ تموتُ الجهاتْ.

ويُطْبِقُ ... حتى النباتْ.

وأنا ليس لي غيرُ أشواقيَ الهامداتْ.

ونزوعٌ شحيحٌ إلى رجْفة للشتاء الذي أطفأتْني أكاذيبُهُ.

لا أُصدِّقُ مِمّا أرى غيرَ يأسي،

أراهُ هنا وهنالك ، أصفرَ ، مِلْءَ الشوارعِ،

بين البيوتِ ، على الشجراتْ.

لا أُصدِّقُ ... أين الفلاةْ؟

وأين امتدادُ الفيافي؟

وأين الجبالُ ، الذُّرى الهائماتْ؟

لا أُصدِّقُ غيرَ انكماشي ويأسي،

وذاك الشتاءُ الذي أطفأتْني أكاذيبُهُ ماتْ.

هنا ترقصُ التُّرَّهاتْ.

هنا فوق هذا المكانِ الذي يكْفَهِرُّ تموتُ الجهاتْ.

ويُطْبِقُ ... حتى النباتْ.

(آذار 1996)

Acknowledgements

An earlier version of "How Long This Day of Mine" appeared in *The Marlboro Review*.

The translators would like to thank Roger Allen, Forrest Gander, and the staff at BOA Editions, for their advice and assistance.

About the Author

Jawdat Fakhreddine was born in 1953 in a small village in south Lebanon. He has published more than ten collections of poetry, the first in 1979. Some of these collections are *Awham rifiyya* (Rural Illusion, 1980), *Manaraton lil ghariq* (Lighthouse for the Drowning, 1996), *Samawat* (Skies, 2002), *Laysa ba'd* (Not Yet, 2006), and *Ḥadiqat al-sittin* (The Garden of Sixty, 2016). He has published two books of literary theory: *Shakl al-qasida al-arabiyya fi al-naqd al-'arabi ḥatta al-qarn al-thamin al-Hijri* (The Form of the Arabic Poem in Arabic Criticism until the Eight Century of the Hijra, 1984) and *al-Iyqa' wa al-zaman: kitabat fi al-naqd al-shi'ri* (Rhythm and Time: Writings in Poetry Criticism, 1995). His articles and poems regularly appear in a number of Lebanese and Arab newspapers. His collection of poems for children titled *Thalathun qasida lil-atfal* (Thirty Poems for Children, 2013) won the Sheikh Zayed Book award in 2014. He is also Professor of Arabic Literature and Criticism at the Lebanese University, Beirut.

About the Translators

Huda Fakhreddine is Assistant Professor of Arabic Literature at the University of Pennsylvania. Her work focuses on modernist movements and trends in Arabic poetry and their relationship to the Arabic literary tradition. She is the author of *Metapoesis in the Arabic Tradition* (Brill, 2015), a study of the modernist poetry of the twentieth century Free Verse movement and the Abbasid *muḥdath* movement, as periods of literary crisis and metapoetic reflection. She holds an MA in English Literature from the American University of Beirut and a PhD in Near Eastern Languages and Civilizations from Indiana University, Bloomington.

Jayson Iwen is a poet and cross-genre writer, the author of *Six Trips in Two Directions* (2006), which won the Emergency Press International Book Award; *A Momentary Jokebook* (2008), which won the Cleveland State University Ruthanne Wiley Memorial Novella Award; and the antinovel *Gnarly Wounds* (2013). Recently published poems of his can be found in *The &Now Awards 3: The Best Innovative Writing*, *Painted Bride Quarterly*, and *Eureka Literary Magazine*. He currently lives in Duluth, Minnesota, and is Associate Professor of Writing at The University of Wisconsin–Superior. He met both Huda and Jawdat Fakhreddine when he lived in Lebanon, where, amongst other things, he was Assistant Professor of English Literature at The American University of Beirut and organizer of the first postwar, open mic reading series in Lebanon.

The Lannan Translations Selection Series

Ljuba Merlina Bortolani, *The Siege*
Olga Orozco, *Engravings Torn from Insomnia*
Gérard Martin, *The Hiddenness of the World*
Fadhil Al-Azzawi, *Miracle Maker*
Sándor Csoóri, *Before and After the Fall: New Poems*
Francisca Aguirre, *Ithaca*
Jean-Michel Maulpoix, *A Matter of Blue*
Willow, Wine, Mirror, Moon: Women's Poems from Tang China
Felipe Benítez Reyes, *Probable Lives*
Ko Un, *Flowers of a Moment*
Paulo Henriques Britto, *The Clean Shirt of It*
Moikom Zeqo, *I Don't Believe in Ghosts*
Adonis (Ali Ahmad Sa'id), *Mihyar of Damascus, His Songs*
Maya Bejerano, *The Hymns of Job and Other Poems*
Novica Tadić, *Dark Things*
Praises & Offenses: Three Women Poets of the Dominican Republic
Ece Temelkuran, *Book of the Edge*
Aleš Šteger, *The Book of Things*
Nikola Madzirov, *Remnants of Another Age*
Carsten René Nielsen, *House Inspections*
Jacek Gutorow, *The Folding Star and Other Poems*
Marosa di Giorgio, *Diadem*
Zeeshan Sahil, *Light and Heavy Things*
Sohrab Sepehri, *The Oasis of Now*
Dariusz Sośnicki, *The World Shared: Poems*
Nguyen Phan Que Mai, *The Secret of Hoa Sen*
Aleš Debeljak, *Smugglers*
Erez Bitton, *You Who Cross My Path*
Mangalesh Dabral, *This Number Does Not Exist*
Knuts Skujenieks, *Seed in Snow*
Jawdat Fakhreddine, *Lighthouse for the Drowning*

For more on the Lannan Translations Selection Series
visit our website:
www.boaeditions.org